Hilary Read

D1759492

The best initial assessment guide

Getting it right – from the start

WITHDRAWN FROM STOCKPORT COLLEGE LEARNING CENTRE

READ ON
PUBLICATIONS LTD

146502

Copyright © Hilary Read and Jane Wells, 2013

The right of Hilary Read and Jane Wells to be identified as the Authors of the Work has been asserted in accordance with the Copyright, Designs and Patents Act 1988.

All rights reserved. No part of this publication may be reproduced, stored in a retrieval system or transmitted in any form or by any means, electronic, mechanical, photocopying, recording or otherwise without prior written permission of Read On Publications Ltd. This text may not be lent, resold, hired out or otherwise disposed of by way of trade in any other form, binding or cover other than that in which it is published without prior consent of the copyright holders.

The publisher has made every reasonable effort to trace the copyright holders of material in this book. Any errors or omissions should be notified in writing to the publisher, who will endeavour to rectify the situation for any reprints and future editions.

First published in the UK in 2013 by

Read On Publications Limited
PO Box 162
Bideford
EX39 9DP

www.readonpublications.co.uk

ISBN 978-1-872678-28-3

Acknowledgements

Grateful thanks go to the following people for their contributions to the guide:

Carol Burrows, Sally Garbett, John Harradence, Colette O'Hagen Ellis, John Plummer Associates, John Skipworth, Judith Ward, Sue Wroe

Photography by James Barke, Bristol, and Ariam Media
Graphic design by Eatcake Design, Bristol
Edited by Sarah Chapman, Bristol
Printed by Toptown Printers Limited, Barnstaple

The best initial assessment guide updates and follows on from *Excellence in initial assessment* (H. Read and J. Wells, 2004). Updates include: RPL and credit transfer; learning theory underpinning initial assessment; links to the national occupational standards; making the business case for IA and links to inspection. Quotes and examples have also been updated, and new material has been added to reflect recent changes.

Other books by Hilary Read

The best assessor's guide
The best quality assurer's guide
Excellence in planning and delivering learning

These are available from
Read On Publications Limited
PO Box 162
Bideford
EX39 9DP

To order by phone, ring the orderline on 0844 888 7138

To buy online, go to www.readonpublications.co.uk

Contents

Foreword

 In the ever-changing environment of FE and training, it is imperative that all stakeholders are up to date with the latest external influences and policies that affect how we develop what we do to meet the needs of all our learners. This new guide, a companion volume to *The best assessor's guide* and *The best quality assurer's guide*, provides an authoritative view of what is now considered to be best initial assessment (IA) practice. Using expert critique from both practitioners and occupational psychologists in the field, it tells you how to set up a high-quality IA process that benefits everyone involved in the learning cycle, while meeting the needs and expectations of your learners.

Ofsted's latest Common Inspection Framework (2012) provides a much-needed re-focus on teaching, learning and assessment. The funding changes that come into force in 2013 provide a clear need to retain our learners for the full length of their planned learning programme. It is therefore vital that IA is carried out thoroughly – without it, learners will be less likely to be on the right programme and more likely to leave without completing it. A poor IA process may also mean that your organisation loses out to the competition and so, with this in mind, the guide also aims to help you make the business case for carrying out high-quality initial assessment.

Hilary Read's previous guides on assessment and quality assurance provide a clear, concise and easy-to-read quick-reference source for everyone involved in the delivery and assessment of vocational learning, by showing how to deliver the latest national occupational standards in practice. These guides have proved invaluable to staff and managers within our organisation in helping drive up the quality of what we deliver.

This latest book in the series continues the theme of providing an expert guide to best practice, to help ensure that the *right learner* is matched up to the *right course*. Robust initial assessment is where the learner starts and, along with effective information, advice and guidance (IAG), will put them on the right road to success if conducted in the right manner. Providing consistency and rigour at this crucial stage should improve retention and therefore the overall performance data of any provider of education and training. Most importantly, it will lead to learners who are motivated and challenged to achieve what is right for them individually.

Mark Care,
Quality Assurance Manager, Lincoln College
('outstanding' for overall effectiveness, Ofsted 2011)

Introduction

If you want to find out more about initial assessment (IA) and what it involves, this guide is for you. It tells you what you need to know about where initial assessment fits within the cycle of learning and development, and how it informs learning programmes and affects the performance of your learners.

You may think that putting together an effective system of initial assessment is complicated and time-consuming, but it can be a straightforward process if you follow the steps outlined here. This guide will also give you the knowledge and skills you need to be able to make an effective commercial case to your managers that initial assessment is worth doing as well as possible, following best practice.

This section describes the benefits of initial assessment and why it is such an important part of learning programmes. It also tells you who the guide is for and how it's structured. It then explains the key principles that form the basis of good practice in initial assessment.

What are the benefits of effective initial assessment?

Having a good initial assessment system brings several benefits:

1 Learners will be better equipped to reach sound decisions about their learning programmes.

2 It will help them – and you – to make sure they have chosen the right programme.

3 It will show them – and you – what they already know and can do and what they still need to learn.

4 It will save your organisation time and money, because you will avoid re-teaching them what they already know or can do.

Initial assessment, based on the six key principles described on the next page, should therefore be an integral part of your recruitment and induction processes. It should also inform the planning of every learner's individual learning programme (ILP). Accurate initial assessment will lead to tighter planning and targeting of learning provision, which in turn will result in better retention and achievement rates.

Good initial assessment (IA) and effective learning plans are essential elements of all learning programmes, including:

- work-based learning
- apprenticeships
- programmes for getting people back into work or training
- rehabilitation programmes
- vocational provision in higher education
- on-job training and development for employees.

Definitions

National occupational standards (NOS) are developed by approved bodies and describe what a person needs to do, know and understand in a job to carry out their role in a consistent and competent way.

Qualifications are certificated by awarding organisations when learners achieve the appropriate requirements by demonstrating knowledge, understanding and/ or their ability to do something.

Who this guide is for

This guide is for everyone with responsibility for the initial assessment of learners. You may be:

- a teacher, trainer or assessor
- a manager
- a union learning representative
- working in higher education
- working towards a qualification, such as:
  - Information, Advice and Guidance (IAG) qualifications, levels 3 or 4
  - an initial teaching qualification
  - the Matrix Standard
  - an assessor qualification.

You may be responsible for one or more of the following:

- recruiting learners to training and learning programmes
- designing or planning learning programmes
- improving retention and achievement rates
- making funding claims for learning
- ensuring that these are in line with learners' previous achievements.

Key principles

Six key principles form the basis of good practice in initial assessment, as shown in the table below.

1	All those with responsibility for initial assessment know exactly what its purpose is and how to carry it out effectively.	This means: • having policies and procedures in place and communicating these to staff • training staff to use a range of IA methods and how to use the information gained from the process to plan learning programmes • making sure that staff explain to learners the purpose of IA and what it involves • using initial assessment methods that are valid, fair and reliable.
2	Initial assessment puts the learner at the centre of the IA process and involves them at every stage.	This means: • not seeing IA as something that is 'done to' the learner • focusing on the learner and their needs (not 'ticking boxes') • tailoring the IA process to meet individual needs and circumstances • taking account of learners' previous learning, achievements and/or experience • having a variety of methods at your disposal and using them with each learner over a period of time (effective IA is not something that can happen within a two-hour slot) • taking account of the learner's opinions, needs, beliefs and preferences.
3	The results of IA are used actively to inform the ILP planning process.	This means: • communicating the results of IA to those involved in the planning process • feeding back the results of IA to learners • knowing what options are available and how to communicate these clearly to learners • working with learners so that they agree with the plan and are keen to follow it.
4	The initial assessment process is open, honest and transparent.	This means: • all parties, including learners, are clear about the purpose of IA and what it involves • having an IA policy that promotes equality of opportunity • making appropriate arrangements to ensure that all those who need to can access the results of IA, while complying with the Data Protection Act 1998 • using methods that are fair and open to scrutiny • meeting the appropriate legal requirements • evaluating your IA procedures regularly and acting on the results.
5	You identify all learners' learning and support needs in relation to the type and length of their programme, and ensure that these needs are met.	This means: • building relationships with learners • taking account of factors that affect learning.
6	The IA process takes account of what learners already know and can do.	This means: • having in place a robust process for recognising prior learning (RPL) • ensuring that everyone involved understands how credit transfer works • making sure that learners don't repeat learning unnecessarily.

What's in the guide?

The guide contains the following chapters:

1: Getting started

This chapter tells you where initial assessment fits within the learning and development cycle. It shows you how to identify your values and write an effective IA policy that recognises learners' existing learning (called recognising prior learning, or RPL).

2: Designing initial assessment

This explains the components that go into an initial assessment system.

3: Choosing and using initial assessment methods

This describes the different methods, the advantages and disadvantages of each and when to use them.

4: Using initial assessment to plan learning

This tells you how to use the results of initial assessment to plan an individual learning programme (ILP) with learners.

5: Keeping it legal

This explains the impact of legislation on initial assessment and planning learning programmes.

6: Making the business case for IA

This shows you how to make the business case for initial assessment to managers, by showing the links to inspection and how this forms part of your overall QA procedures.

Links to national occupational standards (NOS)

Throughout the guide you will find reference to the national occupational standards (NOS) for learning and development, on which initial teacher training qualifications are based.

Activity: *Getting the most from this guide*

Use the following check questions to pinpoint areas where you need to do more work on your present IA policy and procedures. You are aiming to answer yes in each case. Where you answer no, turn to the relevant section of the guide for more help.

Question	Yes	No	Not sure	Turn to page
1 Do we have formal procedures for initial assessment?	☐	☐	☐	11
2 Do we have a written policy?	☐	☐	☐	12
3 If we do, does it include recognition of learners' prior learning (and credit transfer, if we offer QCF qualifications)?	☐	☐	☐	25, 57
4 Do the following people know about our IA policy and procedures?				19
• learners	☐	☐	☐	
• staff	☐	☐	☐	
• parents (where appropriate)	☐	☐	☐	
• employers	☐	☐	☐	
• schools/careers advice staff	☐	☐	☐	
• others	☐	☐	☐	
5 Do we know how to use each of the following methods of initial assessment in ways that are valid, reliable and fair?				41
• interviews	☐	☐	☐	
• psychometric tests	☐	☐	☐	
• in-house designed tests	☐	☐	☐	
• self-assessment questionnaires and checklists	☐	☐	☐	
• observation of group activities	☐	☐	☐	
• application forms	☐	☐	☐	
• recognition of previous learning (including credit transfer and RPL, where appropriate)	☐	☐	☐	
• work experience and work tasters	☐	☐	☐	
6 Do we use the results of IA to plan learning?	☐	☐	☐	67
7 Does our IA system comply with current legislation?	☐	☐	☐	87
8 Is our IA system covered by our organisation's QA procedures (including those we use for internal quality assurance of assessment)?	☐	☐	☐	99
9 Do we continually introduce and monitor improvements linked to our organisation's business objectives?	☐	☐	☐	102

1 Getting started

A growing body of evidence shows that organisations taking a comprehensive approach to IA have higher rates of retention and achievement than those that don't. Putting together an effective initial assessment system is therefore well worth the effort. It's not just the learner who benefits – your organisation will, too.

This section describes the ideal initial assessment system and the best way to go about setting up your own system.

These are the steps you will need to take:

1 Identify your aims, your values and the purposes of initial assessment.

2 Write a policy explaining your approach and procedures.

3 Design your initial assessment system by constructing a flow chart and documenting your key procedures.

4 Pilot and evaluate your system.

5 Make adjustments and implement them.

6 Feed the results of your evaluation into your QA system, monitor improvements and take further action if necessary.

Where does initial assessment fit?

A good initial assessment process should tell you two things:

- where the learner is at the start of any learning and development programme

- where their learning needs lie.

The length of their programme will determine how much initial assessment learners will need. The Qualifications and Curriculum Framework QCF allows training programmes to vary in length, and many learners do 'bite-sized' learning rather than achieving whole qualifications. Your IA system will succeed only if it allows you to gather accurate information about each learner. You need to know what you are looking for at the recruitment stage, and IA will tell you whether your learners fulfil your criteria and enable you to put together an appropriate programme for each learner.

The following table shows how initial assessment can inform learning and assessment at key stages of the learner's programme.

Key point

It's important to see initial assessment as an ongoing process that takes place over a period of time, and not as something done only once with the learner just before they join you.

Stage	Initial assessment will...
1 Recruitment	• ensure that the learner is recruited to the right programme
2 Planning learning	• identify areas the learner needs to develop and the best ways of providing learning and development • show the learner what they need to do – if they don't know what they have to do, how can they be expected to achieve anything?
3 Induction	• show the learner where they may need particular help or support; in other words, make initial assessment an integral part of the induction process
4 Learning and development	• show the learner how far they have progressed as a result of the learning and development they have undergone
5 Assessment planning	• highlight existing achievements that show the learner what they still need to learn. You need this information if you are to plan successfully for summative assessment.

Towards an IA policy

Setting out your aims and procedures for IA in a written policy will ensure that all members of staff, learners, parents and potential employers can understand what initial assessment involves and what you are trying to achieve.

What are our values?

Before you start to set out your own policy, ask yourself about your values. What are you promoting with your learners? What matters most to your organisation? By identifying your core values, you will have identified the starting point for your initial assessment policy. For example, one organisation decided that its values were 'to identify and respond to what individuals can already do at the start of their programmes and to provide them with a clear understanding of what they need to do to achieve their goals and targets.' This would be a good aim for any initial assessment system.

Here are some more examples of aims and values set by training providers:

- 'We put the learner at the centre of everything we do.'
- 'Our company's mission is to identify every learner's strengths and to build on them.'
- 'We respect individuality and the differing needs of learners.'
- 'We aim to include the learner in all aspects of their learning.'
- 'We encourage all trainees to achieve their maximum potential.'
- 'Our organisation values honesty and openness.'
- 'We aim to be at the heart of the community.'
- 'We aim to maintain learners' dignity.'
- 'We are champions of equal opportunity in all areas of learning.'
- 'We value all learners' strengths and encourage their capability to learn and develop.'

Initial, formative and summative assessment: a reminder

Three main types of assessment underpin learning and development:

1 **Initial assessment** is the process of assessing the learner's needs, capability and potential at the beginning of a programme. This information then informs the learner's individual learning plan and what they need to be taught.

2 **Formative assessment** is an ongoing process that takes place as the learner is learning. The teacher or trainer assesses the learner's progress towards their learning goals and gives them feedback on their progress, including what they need to do to improve.

3 **Summative assessment** usually takes place when formative assessment has done its job and the learner is ready to have their performance and/or what they know finally assessed – for example, against the assessment criteria contained within the QCF qualification(s) they are aiming to achieve.

Policy elements

Some of the elements worth including in an IA policy come under the following headings.

Aims

This should be a short statement outlining what you are aiming to achieve as a result of IA.

Key procedures

It's useful to show your key procedures in the form of a diagram such as a flow chart.

Individual learning plans (ILPs)

Set out your approach to ILPs, for example:

- how the areas you initially assess link to the ILP
- links to RPL and credit transfer, if relevant.

'A short training programme often won't need a lengthy initial assessment. In such cases we put learners through a skills check and ask them on the registration forms if they have any learning difficulties or support needs. We generally put them on to the IOSH Working Safely course first, which does require some writing, and, if they need help, this information is passed on to the teacher or assessor responsible. Those undertaking longer programmes such as apprenticeships get a far more lengthy and rigorous initial and diagnostic assessment.'

Training manager

IA methods

Include a a brief description of the methods you use (or intend to use), including:

- how they will be used and over what period of time
- who will use them.

Use of the results

You should say what you do with the results of IA in relation to:

- planning ILPs
- providing learning and development – the options available to learners and how you can provide them
- recording, storing and communicating the results.

IA and the law

Describe the procedures you use in terms of how they comply with current legislation.

Other information

This should include:

- the name of the person responsible for initial assessment and individual learning plans
- the training or knowledge required to carry out IA
- an annual review date
- the QA procedures you intend to use to evaluate the effectiveness of your IA policy and procedures, including people, resources, timescales and review dates.

Writing your own policy: top tips

Here are some tips to help you when you are writing your own initial assessment policy.

- Use the sample policy shown on the next two pages as a guide to the layout of your own policy, adapting it as appropriate to your own organisation.

- Use a flowchart to document your procedures graphically. This gives readers a visual and quick way to gain a picture of the whole process. Use the example shown on page 17 as a template help you to create your own.

- Keep your policy brief: two or three sides of A4 at most.

- Include examples of the initial assessment instruments you use, such as tests and self-assessment checks, as appendices to your main policy. Try to include everything you use as part of the IA process.

- To make sure you leave nothing out as you write your policy, imagine you are explaining your approach and procedures to a new member of staff.

- Since your aim is for everyone to understand the policy, use short sentences and plain language. Explain any jargon or acronyms in footnotes or brackets as you go.

- Get someone else to read through your draft and comment on whether it is easy to understand and whether or not you have included everything. Change it or add to it as a result of what they say.

A sample policy

The next two pages show how one training provider set out its IA policy.

The Best Training Provider

Initial assessment policy

1 Policy statement

At The Best Training Provider, we aim to identify each learner's goals and aspirations accurately and guide them to the appropriate course and programme. We will refer learners to other providers if we are unable to meet their needs.

2 Aim

The purpose of our initial assessment is to gather sufficient information to enable us to design a learning plan that reflects the learner's specific needs and ensure that they have the best opportunity to attain their learning goals. We aim to ensure that each learner has a positive experience and achieves their potential.

2.1 Individual Learning Plan

When identifying what a learner needs, to enable them to learn and achieve, we will consider:

2.1.1 their career aspirations and their relevant abilities and skills

2.1.2 the most appropriate learning programme for them

2.1.3 what they have already learnt and know:

- whether they have proof or not via our RPL process

- any credits they bring with them via credit transfer.

3 Administration and standards

3.1 Initial assessment process

The initial assessment process will be comprehensive and it will gather information about each learner's:

3.1.1 career aspirations and interests

3.1.2 qualifications and achievements

3.1.3 aptitude and potential

3.1.4 recognition of prior learning

3.1.5 basic literacy and numeracy learning needs

3.1.6 learning difficulties

3.1.7 learning styles

3.1.8 personal circumstances that may affect learning and achievement.

3.2 Data Protection Act 1998

We will ensure that all our initial assessment activities comply with the relevant legislation with regard to data protection, by gaining learners' signed permission to collect and share information with appropriate others and keeping electronic records securely, password protected, and accessed by named individuals only.

3.3 Equality of opportunity legislation

We will ensure that all our activities comply with the relevant legislation with regard to equality of opportunity, which is:

- the Human Rights Act 1998

- the Equality Act 2010

3.4 Our approach to initial assessment

We will ensure that learners:

3.4.1 are fully involved in the initial assessment process

3.4.2 understand the benefits of what they are being asked to do and how the information will be used

3.4.3 agree how recommendations on learning requirements will be met

3.4.4 receive feedback that is positive and encouraging

3.4.5 can give their views, and that these are collected and recorded

3.4.6 receive initial assessment methods that are appropriate

3.4.7 are subject to assessment methods that are effective and do not discriminate against them

3.4.8 receive an individual summary that records the outcomes of their initial assessment and is used to design their learning plan.

4 Staff skills and experience

4.1 Training

All staff carrying out initial assessment will be appropriately trained. All staff will have attended XYZ's interview skills course, be up to date with QCF practice, and will be working towards an appropriate teacher training qualification.

Person responsible	Date of policy	Review date
Ellie Hughes	16 April 2013	15 April 2014

A sample flowchart

Use a flowchart similar to this to show your IA process in a visual way.

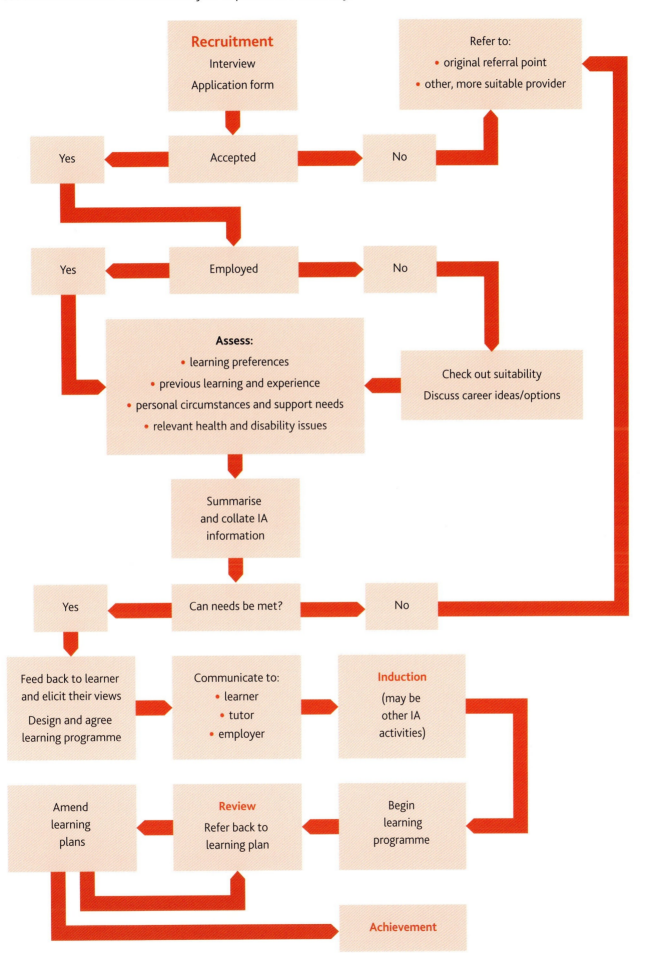

2 Designing initial assessment

Clearly, initial assessment should be useful and enjoyable for all your learners, and designed to encourage and motivate them to learn. To ensure that learners are going to enjoy the process, it will need to include a variety of interesting activities, spread over a period of time. Most people enjoy finding out about themselves and their abilities and preferences; they like answering questionnaires and appreciate getting feedback on their responses.

The way you design your initial assessment system will also depend on the particular context and needs of your learners and the other people or organisations involved. This chapter considers initial assessment in the wider context and then explains its main components. It tells you how to assess a learner's:

- occupational suitability

- occupational and technical skills

- personal skills

- basic and functional skills

- learning and study skills

- learning support needs

- health and ability.

This chapter also explains relevant learning theories and how they apply to IA.

Initial assessment in context

The methods you use and the topics you cover in your initial assessment system will depend to a large extent on the learning programmes you offer and your learners' personal objectives. However, there are several general points to bear in mind when you design your initial assessment system.

You will need to take account of:

- **the context in which learners learn.** For example, assessing someone initially in the workplace is different from assessing them within an educational institution.

- **industry standards and regulatory requirements.** For example, some employer programmes have rigorous entry requirements and some qualifications require you to have certain procedures and processes in place to satisfy regulatory requirements.

- **the support needs of learners.** This means considering any individual help they are likely to need, to give them the best chance of succeeding.

- **your existing resources.** These include people, time and equipment.

Think about whether your IA system needs to include assessment of some or all of the following:

- occupational suitability and expectations

- occupational and technical skills

- learners' existing skills and knowledge – including recognition of prior learning (RPL) and credit transfer, where appropriate

- basic and functional skills – literacy, language and numeracy; functional maths; functional English; functional ICT

- personal skills, such as team-working and communication

- learning support needs

- health checks.

If your organisation is responsible for providing more than one type of programme or more than one occupation, using a table like the one opposite is a useful way to ensure that everyone involved knows what needs to be done. The table lists examples of learning programmes and shows what you might include in initial assessment for that programme.

Tailoring IA to learners' programmes

Programme	Certificate or qualification	Programme length	IA includes assessment of...
Short courses, such as those designed to get people back into work	Certificate of achievement and attendance; qualification in literacy/numeracy; a one- or two-unit QCF award	One to six weeks	• occupational suitability • literacy/numeracy skills • learning support needs, with emphasis on personal circumstances such as health or disability issues that affect learning • personal skills
E-learning	Knowledge required for European Computer Driving Licence	Flexible to suit the needs of the learner, for example two to three hours per week, negotiated with each learner	• basic skills • previous ICT knowledge and experience • access to ICT resources at home • suitability of delivery packages • health or disability issues that affect learning
Apprenticeships	Apprenticeship framework: QCF qualification(s) at level 2 or 3; functional skills and personal learning and thinking skills (PLTS)	18 months to 3 years	• occupational suitability • occupational and technical skills (within certain occupational areas) • functional skills • personal skills - PLTS • learning support needs • health and disability in the context of the occupational area • RPL • credit transfer
In-house work-based training aimed at employees	QCF level 2 in Business Administration	Three to nine months	• occupational and technical skills • RPL • credit transfer • basic skills • learning preferences
Vocational courses within higher education	Diploma in Nursing	Three years	• occupational suitability • basic skills • learning support needs • health issues as they apply to nursing

Assessing occupational suitability

An important part of initial assessment on vocational courses is assessing occupational suitability. Doing this in the early stages will save you time and money in the long run, as learners will drop out if they find they are working in an occupation that doesn't suit them.

Assessing expectations

Have you ever started a course and left within the first few weeks? If this has happened to you, it was probably because your expectations were not met. Your starting point is therefore to investigate expectations.

Read the quote on the right and think about the learner's expectations. In this example involving a young person, it was the learning provider who failed to manage her expectations from the word go.

It is important to make sure that the learners' perceptions and expectations are realistic. Their reasons for choosing a particular occupation aren't always the right ones. They may lack experience if they are young, as in the example above. They can sometimes base their career decisions on unreliable sources of information such as TV programmes. (For example, TV programmes such as *Call the Midwife* and *One born every minute* may influence prospective recruits on to midwifery courses, while *CSI* has influenced a growing interest in forensic science.) Added to this, peers, parents or teachers may unduly influence learners' decisions. As a consequence, many have unrealistic career expectations.

'I signed up for a Health and Social Care apprenticeship. No one told me how long the shifts would be, or about the personal care side with the residents. I found it really upsetting when one of them died, and I left after a few weeks.'

Learner

Methods to use

You can assess expectations effectively by constructing quizzes or by using more formal assessment methods.

Using online assessment to manage expectations

One university found that applicants to nursing training had inaccurate ideas about what they would be doing on a day-to-day basis or what they would be studying. Their solution was to commission a professionally constructed questionnaire designed to gauge prospective nurses' expectations. After completing the assessment, individuals scored their own questionnaire, thus cognitively processing accurate career information for themselves. This approach significantly reduced the early leaver rate.

The main initial assessment methods used to assess occupational suitability are:

- career guidance tests or assessments

- work tasters or structured work experience

- discussion of hobbies, interests and career ideas.

Career guidance tests or assessments

Many career guidance tests and assessments are available. Traditionally, they ask respondents to choose between work characteristics that are then linked to particular careers or occupations. The theory underpinning this type of assessment has been influential since the early 1970s, when John Holland[1] identified that people in similar jobs often have similar skills and interests. These similarities can be grouped around:

- data – such as facts and figures

- ideas – such as thinking about new ways of doing things

- people – such as jobs with a social focus

- things - such as working with machines and equipment.

The following table shows some of the strengths and weaknesses associated with these tests and assessments. You need to weigh them up before deciding whether or not to add them to your initial assessment system.

Strengths	Weaknesses
<ul><li>Structured</li><li>Comprehensive</li><li>Easy to use</li><li>Based on careful research; robust and reliable</li></ul>	<ul><li>They may focus on the tasks and skills of groups of jobs rather than the day-to-day realities and difficulties of specific jobs</li><li>You may need access to IT and/or the internet before you can use them</li><li>Staff need specific training</li><li>Can be expensive</li></ul>

Work tasters

Work tasters are real-life, structured experiences set up within the workplace. They provide a context for assessing someone's suitability for working in a particular occupation. Volunteering is one way of gaining insight and experience, particularly for the unemployed, as it does not affect their benefits. However, this is appropriate only if it fits with the individual's career aspirations.

The following table shows the strengths and weaknesses of work tasters.

Strengths	Weaknesses
<ul><li>Can put right learners' inaccurate perceptions or expectations</li><li>Can reduce early leaver rates</li><li>Popular with learners if they are clearly related to the jobs they are interested in</li></ul>	<ul><li>Tend to be expensive to develop and use</li><li>Active support of employers needed to make them work</li><li>Resource-intensive if used extensively</li></ul>

See Chapter 3 for more information on choosing and using work tasters.

---

[1] Holland, J. L., *Making Vocational Choices: a Theory of Careers* (Englewood Cliffs, NJ: Prentice Hall, 1973)

Discussion of hobbies, interests and career ideas

Discussing the learner's hobbies and interests can be useful if you have a good knowledge of the occupational area the learner wishes to enter. You need to prepare for this so that you ask good-quality, appropriate questions. If you are considering using discussion as part of initial assessment, you need to be trained in interviewing and qualified to provide advice and guidance on careers and learning.

Be aware, however, that learners sometimes fail to divulge their real hobbies and interests. They may feel intimidated, embarrassed or just forget to mention something on the day. You can reduce this risk if you can establish a good rapport with the learner before exploring more personal issues.

You also need to be careful that your discussions do not infringe learners' rights to privacy under the Human Rights Act 1998. This means planning what questions you will ask of everyone and ensuring that your questions are relevant and not too intrusive. (See Chapter 5 for more on the relevant legislation.)

'While I was receiving benefits, I signed up for a learndirect course at my local ICT centre. I thought I was going along to become computer literate. Instead, I found I had to pass an exam and that the provider didn't get all their funding unless I did. No one told me this until I was well into the modules, and then only because I was taking my time – or "falling behind" – as the tutor put it. I hadn't taken an exam in years and I felt pressured, so I left.'

Learner

Assessing occupational and technical skills

Some craft and technical occupations, such as engineering or construction, require particular skills and abilities. This means that initial assessment must assess learners' potential in key areas such as:

- mechanical reasoning
- spatial awareness
- manual dexterity.

The results will show the extent to which learners may have to develop these skills and abilities in order to achieve their qualifications or learning outcomes.

Taking account of existing skills and knowledge

Identifying what learners already know and can already do plays a major part in motivating them to participate in further learning or development. Learners will become discouraged if they have to repeat learning activities or experiences during the course of their programmes.

Here are some general things to look for:

- Ask young learners about what they have already done as part of their schooling or further education experience. Be open to the fact that it may well be different from your own or your staff's experiences. For example, many learners leave school with ICT qualifications. Ask them, too, about Saturday or holiday jobs.

- Ask those who have been outside mainstream education about their life experiences. Looking after children or siblings, living within a budget, running clubs, working as a volunteer and DIY are all valid experiences and vehicles for learning.

- Find out whether the learner has started a previous training course and left early, as they may have existing knowledge of topics such as health and safety.

Much of the prospective learner's previous knowledge and experience may not have been documented or accredited. However, recognising and exploring it with the learner will not only underline the message that all learning is valuable but will also motivate them to continue.

Recognition of prior learning (RPL)

Providers of QCF qualifications must have a formal RPL process in place for learners who wish to have evidence of their knowledge and performance assessed and recognised against the learning outcomes and assessment criteria within existing units and qualifications. The RPL process was introduced originally to widen access to assessment for those who might not have undertaken formal programmes of learning, and means that learners don't have to repeat learning unnecessarily.[2]

---

[2] *Claiming credit: Guidance on the recognition of prior learning within the Qualifications and Credit Framework, Version 2* (Qualifications and Curriculum Authority, 2010)

'We started recruiting engineering apprentices based on their A-level results, but found that drop-out rates increased. The reason was that we'd placed more emphasis on intellectual than manual ability. We've since re-introduced the manual dexterity tests as a condition of recruitment.'

Centre manager, engineering

Remember

1 RPL impacts on the way in which you deliver learning. People undergoing RPL won't need to do everything you provide.

2 RPL is not the same as credit transfer, because it involves summative assessment of what the learner can already do or already knows. (Credit transfer is where the learner already has credits and transfers them straight into the qualification.)

3 In terms of the learning journey, RPL means that the learner can go straight for summative assessment in areas where you agree that they can show they are already competent.

RPL includes assessment of:

- experience
- learning
- achievements.

In essence, RPL means giving learners advice and guidance on whether or not they already possess evidence that is valid, authentic, reliable and sufficient. This is assessed in the normal way. If you are a qualified assessor, you will probably already do this as part of initial assessment. If not, you will need to involve an assessor at the recruitment and initial assessment stages of your programmes. RPL consists of six stages.[3]

The six stages of RPL

Stage 1: General information, advice and guidance (IAG) about claiming credit

Here you give the learner information, advice and guidance about the process for claiming credit to enable them to make a decision about whether or not to use the RPL route, as there are usually time and resource implications in doing so.

Stage 2: Pre-assessment

Once the learner decides to claim credit through RPL, you'll need to draw up a detailed assessment plan against the requirements of the unit(s). They don't have to claim for a full unit: learners are much more likely to have evidence that only partially covers the unit. You will need to tell them what they need to provide for assessment purposes.

Stage 3: Assessment/documentation of evidence

When you are assessing evidence as part of RPL, you use the same process for reaching an assessment decision as you would for any other aspect of assessing evidence of knowledge and performance. A suitably qualified and/or occupationally experienced assessor chooses appropriate methods and assesses the evidence of the learner's competence. His or her decision is then subject to internal and external quality procedures in the normal way.

Stage 4: Feedback

After assessment, feedback is given and the results are discussed with the learner to confirm whether or not to award credits, following your centre's normal procedures. This would usually be followed by further support and guidance on the options available.

Stage 5: Awarding credit

The awarding organisation records all credits achieved through RPL in the learner's personal learning record, in exactly the same way as all other credits.

Stage 6: Appealing

Learners wishing to appeal against an assessment decision must follow your centre's standard appeals procedure.

---

[3] See also Read, H., *The best quality assurer's guide* (Read On Publications, 2012)

For more about assessing using appropriate methods, see Read, H., *The best assessor's guide* (Read On Publications, 2011).

Credit transfer

Credit transfer is the process of transferring credits directly from one unit or qualification to another for certification. It means that the learner does not have to repeat either learning or assessment. Similarly, if you are in receipt of government funding, it means that your organisation does not claim for learning and assessment time twice.

Activity: RPL versus credit transfer

This activity is for you if you are responsible for recruiting and initially assessing learners on to programmes that lead to credit-based qualifications under the QCF.

Here are two of the qualifications for internal quality assurers (IQAs) of assessment.

Level 4 Award in understanding the internal quality assurance of assessment processes and practice
This award is for IQAs who carry out internal quality assurance activities on their own.

Unit 4: Understanding the principles and practices of internally assuring the quality of assessment	Unit 5: Internally assure the quality of assessment

Level 4 Certificate in leading the internal quality assurance of assessment processes and practice
The certificate is for lead IQAs who are responsible for a team of IQAs.

Unit 4: Understanding the principles and practices of internally assuring the quality of assessment	Unit 5: Internally assure the quality of assessment	Unit 8: Plan, allocate and monitor work in own area of responsibility

Imagine that you are responsible for the following learners:

Learner 1: This learner has already achieved a level 4 qualification in leadership and management that includes the shared unit: 'Plan, allocate and monitor work in own area of responsibility'. She now wishes to achieve the level 4 QCF Certificate in leading the internal quality assurance of assessment processes and practice.

Learner 2: This learner is already a qualified and practising internal verifier (IV) and holds an NVQ V1 Award. She wants to update to the two-unit Award in the internal quality assurance of assessment processes and practice.

Which process applies in each of these examples – credit transfer or RPL?

Answers on page 29

Assessing personal skills

Personal skills concern our attitudes to and interactions with others. Most people possess these skills in some measure, and yet they can be difficult to identify or assess unless you are clear about what you're looking for.

Other phrases used to describe personal skills include:

- interpersonal skills
- personal learning and thinking skills (PLTS)
- 'soft' skills
- emotional intelligence (EI).

For all occupational areas that involve dealing with others, these skills are critical, as the quotes in the margin illustrate.

In order to know whether or not to assess these skills on entry, you'll need to identify the contexts in which they are important. To find out, you can:

- ask the 'experts': employers, occupational tutors or subject specialists
- ask learners at various stages of their programmes. They will tell you about the personal skills they needed to develop, and why.

Assessing personal learning and thinking skills (PLTS)

PLTS form part of apprenticeship frameworks and comprise generic skills in:

- independent enquiry
- effective participation
- team-working
- self-management
- reflective learning
- creative thinking.

Here are some dos and don'ts when initially assessing PLTS.

Do	Don't
• tell learners about them at the beginning of their programmes	• map them across to the vocational qualification, then forget about them
• initially assess them – informally if necessary – so that learners know that they are part of their entitlement	• take a checklist approach and tick them off as learners 'cover' them: they need to be taught as part of every learner's entitlement
• pass on any information you gain from IA to those responsible for teaching them.	• leave assessment of them until the end of a learner's programme.

'If they are going to work in a nursery, learners need to know how to engage with very young children, such as sitting or kneeling down with them so that they do not intimidate by literally talking down to them.'

'Before learners join our equine training, we ask them to spend a week in the yard so that we can see how they react to the horses – and how the horses react to them.'

'At the hospice, we have a fairly rigorous initial assessment procedure when we employ carers. We had one who said she wasn't expecting to deal with dying people, even though she had all the right qualifications!'

'We run a shelter for the homeless and an advice centre. We expect new people to have an awareness of the issues and empathy with our clients.'

Assessing basic and functional skills

Basic skills are the generic skills that everyone needs in order to carry out everyday tasks. They are:

'…the ability to read, write and speak in English and to use mathematics at a level necessary to function at work and in society in general.'

Improving literacy and numeracy: A fresh start (DfEE, 1999)

Functional skills refer to the ability to apply these generic skills in a practical context.

Basic skills

Basic skills are more commonly known as literacy, language (English for speakers of other languages) and numeracy. Literacy, language and numeracy form part of many learning programmes, such as:

- welfare-to-work courses
- workplace learning
- learning at home or in the community.

Functional skills

Functional skills are:

- Mathematics
- English
- Information and communication technology (ICT).

RPL versus credit transfer: answers

Learner 1: The learner already has a unit worth five credits towards the Certificate, so she would not need to repeat anything – learning or assessment – as she can automatically transfer these credits across, using credit transfer.

Learner 2: This learner would need to present relevant performance and product evidence under your RPL process, to prove that she can still meet the learning outcomes and assessment criteria in the units for which she is claiming credit. Any evidence would then be assessed in the normal way. If she has kept her knowledge and practice up to date, she would not have to undergo any further learning. If she hasn't, you would need to tailor your learning programme to meet her needs (for example, requiring her to attend only the relevant sessions and/or asking a more senior colleague to do some one-to-one coaching).

Functional skills are practical skills, primarily concerned with applying skills in a variety of different contexts to enable learners to deal with practical problems and challenges. Employers often ask for functional skills, and they are seen as the basis on which learners can build their employability skills. Functional skills are a mandatory part of apprenticeships. They are also available as stand-alone qualifications for other learners.

Using online assessment tools

You may decide to use online tools for initial assessment of basic and functional skills. They tend to be rather expensive, however, unless you are a large provider with large numbers of learners. A paper-based one may work just as well, particularly in a work-based environment where an internet signal may be unreliable or non-existent.

It's vital to ensure that learners respond positively to the idea of doing an online initial assessment. You need to explain clearly what the benefits are, and why you are asking them to do the assessment test.

Compare the first two quotes in the margin on the facing page. It's not difficult to see whose learners will be motivated to improve their skills in these areas, and that getting this wrong may well set the tone for the whole learning programme.

Activity: *Choosing a skills assessment tool*

There are many online tools you can use for assessing learners' basic and functional skills initially. You may find the following checklist helpful when researching and using these.

'I tell learners they must know how to read and interpret the decimal point. We deal in milligrams with medication.'

Veterinary nurse trainer

'We don't use online assessment tools as we've not found one we like. They also tend to be rather expensive unless you have large numbers of learners (which is why they may be suitable for larger providers). We've found a paper-based one that works for us, particularly in a work-based environment where an internet signal can be unreliable at best, or even non-existent. This way, we can deliver initial assessments on site for any number of learners in one go.'

Functional skills tutor

My chosen IA tool...	Yes	No
1 builds on what the learner can already do – not what they can't do		
2 is appropriate for the level at which my learners start their programmes		
3 encourages the learner to get involved in their assessment process		
4 avoids formal 'test' conditions that are likely to put learners off		
5 contains questions that are in context, allowing learners to apply them to their own lives and work		
6 gives results that tell me whether or not learners have a realistic chance of succeeding		
7 provides results on which we can base a meaningful learning plan		
8 is designed by a reputable organisation and/or a suitably qualified professional		

You are aiming to answer yes in each case. Where you answer no, move on to another IA tool or take action.

Assessing learning and study skills

Learning and study skills are generic skills that learners need to have if they are to complete a course of study successfully. They are also known as:

- learning to learn skills
- thinking skills
- skills of meta-cognition.

If you offer courses of learning that require learners to have these skills before they start, you need to tell them from the outset. Many courses include modules that introduce learners to these skills, emphasising that they are crucial to their success.

If a learning programme requires learners to organise themselves and their thinking, you will need to gauge at the beginning whether or not your learner is likely to stick at it and succeed. Examples of such programmes are:

- online or 'distance learning' courses with little or no direct contact with the teacher
- those that require learners to produce structured assignments, essays, projects or reports
- those containing standards or assessment criteria that demand high-level cognitive ability from the learner.

Assessing learning support needs

Learners are all individuals with individual experiences and needs. As more people are encouraged to join learning programmes, you will encounter a greater range of needs than in the past. To give each learner the best possible chance of achieving their chosen qualifications or targets, you will have to identify in each case what additional support they may need.

Factors affecting learning

You need to find out what your learners have found helpful and enjoyed in the past, as well as the things that they found difficult, embarrassing or boring. The best way of doing this is to ask them, but it's important to be sensitive about how you do this. Bear in mind that every learner has had different experiences of learning, positive and negative, and that these experiences inform their attitudes.

The diagrams overleaf show how two different learners identified the factors affecting their learning. Examples like these can provide you with a good starting point for further discussion of support for a person's learning.

'I always explain these skills to learners in advance and tell them what I'm looking for at initial assessment. I also make a point of talking positively. I say, "We try very hard to make sure that you enjoy it and there is always someone on hand to help," rather than, "Don't worry, we have special classes for people with reading difficulties like you."'

Literacy teacher

'I took my daughter to a college for a whole afternoon, where large numbers of learners were herded from pillar to post to do online initial assessments in literacy and numeracy. None of them knew what they were doing or why they were doing it. My daughter was distressed by the end, as she didn't think she'd done very well – even though it was clear to me that her scores were fine.'

Parent

'I started an initial teaching qualification at my local FE college. I found I was the only work-based trainer in a group of lecturers, who all seemed to take the assignment work in their stride. I hadn't set foot inside a classroom for 15 years and didn't know where to start.'

Trainee teacher

1 A parent returning to part-time study

Things that help me	Things that stop me
Setting aside time each week	Being interrupted by the children
Telling the family when these times are	Partner using the computer
My love of studying (I look forward to it)	Feeling tired or stressed

2 An apprentice in wood occupations

Things that help me	Things that stop me
I'm good at making things	I don't like the 'theory' side of the job
My dad's a cabinet-maker	I'm not good at talking to people
I enjoy going to work	I don't always take criticism well

Understanding learning preferences

Finding out how learners prefer to learn does not, by itself, help you manage their learning. Research shows that many models of 'learning styles' are in use, but that not all of them are based on valid or reliable information.[4] Inspections also show that many providers use questionnaires to find out about learning styles, but then do nothing with the results.

You need to plan your approach when setting up your initial assessment procedures. Here are some tips:

- Rather than using a one-off, 'learning preferences' model, think instead in terms of starting an ongoing discussion with each learner concerning their best ways of learning or approaching different tasks. You can then follow up the initial conversation each time you review the learner's progress.

- Avoid labelling learners according to their preferred learning style. It's easy to say, for example, 'She's an activist – she likes learning by doing,' or 'He likes reading and studying, so he's a theorist,' and thereby pigeonhole the learner. The best learners are those who can adapt their learning style to the circumstances, so encourage learners to try out new ways of doing things, even if it means that they make mistakes.

'When I run a training session, I try to design it with my target audience in mind. For example, managers are often theorists – you can explain ideas to them and they can think through how they apply. Work-based trainers are more practical – they're doers like their learners, so I include plenty of experiential activities. If I have a mixed group, I'll have a mixture of activities and I'll explain the reasons for this.'

Management trainer

---

4   Coffield, F. et al, *Learning Styles for Post-16 Learners: What do we know?* (LSRC, 2004)

- Be clear about the purpose of initially assessing learning styles or preferences. Ask, 'Why are we doing this?' and, 'What will we do with the results?' Don't raise learners' expectations that they have a choice unless you have the resources to support them and unless you intend to act on what learners say.

- Use the information you gain about learners' preferred ways of doing things to help you improve the quality of teaching and learning within your organisation. Compare what actually happens with the ways in which learners say they prefer to learn, and identify areas where you could make changes or improvements.

Assessing health and ability

Under the Health and Safety at Work Act 1974 you have a legal responsibility to ensure that you protect the health, safety and welfare of all your learners. This means collecting information about them. However, you must consider carefully what information you collect and the reasons for collecting it.

'I signed up for a blended learning course, but left after a couple of months. I love discussion and I expected to share my learning and experiences with other members of the group and to meet up at some point. Instead, I found I had to go through the online tutor and I didn't get to speak to anyone else. After I left, I joined an evening class at my local college. I still gained the qualification I wanted and I also made some new friends.'

Learner

Ask yourself the following questions:

- What are the health and safety reasons for collecting the information?
- Do we really need to know this information?
- What are we going to do with the information?
- What actions will result from having gathered it?
- Who is going to process it and how is it going to be securely stored?
- Do we comply with the requirements of the Data Protection Act 1998? (See Chapter 5 for more information on the Act.)
- Do learners know why the information is being collected?

Asking the right health questions

It's impossible to ask learners about every health condition that may affect their ability to undertake a particular learning programme. Too many physical and psychological conditions exist to allow you to produce a comprehensive health questionnaire. However, you can ask some useful questions at the outset. These can be general or specific, depending on the learner's occupation.

Remember

It's illegal to discriminate on grounds of disability unless you can show that the safety of others is at risk. See Chapter 5 for more information.

A **general question** might be:

Do you have a health issue or disability that may mean that you need additional arrangements or help to enable you to work safely and/or attend a learning centre?

A **specific question** is appropriate for occupations where particular disabilities cannot be supported with 'reasonable adjustments'. For example, in relation to the use of scaffolding in the construction industry, you could ask:

Do you have a health issue or disability that means you may need additional arrangements or help to enable you to work safely at height in the scaffolding industry? For example, do you suffer from uncontrolled vertigo, type-2 diabetes or high blood pressure?

Here are some common health issues associated with different occupations:

Remember

An appropriately qualified nurse or doctor should always carry out health screening.

Health issue	Occupation
Problems with lifting (back injuries)	Land-based industries Care Construction Retail distribution
Contagious illness, allergies	Care Hospitality and catering Hairdressing Working with animals (veterinary, equine)
Epilepsy or migraines	Using computers
Colour blindness	Electrical Design and printing
Fear of confined spaces	Installation (plumbing, gas, water or electrical)

Learning theories: domains and taxonomies

Many learning programmes have entry requirements and/or standards that learners must achieve by the end of their programmes. If you are responsible for assessing and making decisions about whether or not a learner meets your entry requirements – or has the potential to meet them – you'll find it helpful to understand some of the basic learning theories underpinning assessment.

Learning domains

You can link initial assessment of learners' skills, knowledge and attitudes to the three main learning domains: cognitive, psychomotor and affective. Described by the educational theorist Benjamin Bloom (1956), the domains offer a useful way of pointing you to an appropriate method of initial assessment. The domains vary in importance according to the occupational area and the nature of the learning programme.

The table below shows how you can apply the domains within two generic areas that underpin many learning programmes – reflective practice and ethical practice. For each domain, there are two examples of assessment criteria and suggestions for a IA method you might use.

Notice how the verbs change within each domain.

Learning domain and what it means	Assessment criterion	IA method
Cognitive Learners' thinking skills; their knowledge and understanding	Evaluate the effectiveness of different approaches to reflective practice and continuing professional development within own area of responsibility Summarise ways of ensuring that ethical practice is maintained when dealing with individuals and groups face to face or remotely, by telephone or online	Assessing previous learning, experience or achievement Questioning
Psychomotor Learners' physical or 'doing' skills and their ability to put them into practice by performing a task	Maintain a reflective journal in relation to own practice Participate in continuous professional development in order to improve professional competence, knowledge and skills	Observation Work tasters Assessing previous learning, experience or achievement (and non-achievement, as this can prevent further failure).
Affective Learners' attitudes and values: *how* they think and/or apply their skills	Explain the value of reflective practice and continuing professional development in relation to your professional practice Recognise how your own ethics and behaviour appear to other people	Psychometric testing Self-assessment questionnaire Interview Observation of group activity

The importance of the domains varies: for example, the affective domain underpins customer service, whereas aptitude within the psychomotor domain (manual dexterity, mechanical reasoning, spatial awareness, etc.) may be the focal point for some manufacturing jobs.

Evaluate means 'to assess the worth of'.

'Maintain' and 'participate' are active verbs that mean that the learner has to demonstrate their performance.

This domain is less easy to define and is often implicit within the other two. (You could argue that the first criterion also belongs in the cognitive domain, for example.)

To find out more about using the initial assessment methods above, see Chapter 3.

Taxonomies of learning

Taxonomies of learning are another useful tool for defining the level of learning that learners can demonstrate. If you are assessing against entry requirements, you will need to measure what levels of knowledge or performance your learner already possesses. Understanding how taxonomies work will help you do this more effectively.

Taxonomies are designed as hierarchies – the higher up the taxonomy you go, the greater the level of challenge and complexity for the learner.

There are taxonomies in all three learning domains: cognitive, psycho-motor and affective. One of the most widely recognised is Benjamin Bloom's taxonomy, which he and others designed to categorise the level of abstraction in questions commonly used by educators. This taxonomy is concerned with the cognitive domain, that is, knowledge and understanding. It starts with the concrete at the lowest level of demand – knowing and remembering facts – and moves on to more complex and abstract skills – such as the ability to analyse and evaluate information – through to synthesis at the highest level.

The diagram below shows you how verbs within assessment criteria, standards or learning objectives can be linked to Bloom's taxonomy using examples from the national occupational standards (NOS) for Libraries, Archives, Records and Information Management Services (LARIMS).[5]

'We have learners who join at entry-level 2 or below. It is impossible to get them up to level 2 unless the provider is prepared to offer intensive, one-to-one or small group support.'

Functional skills tutor

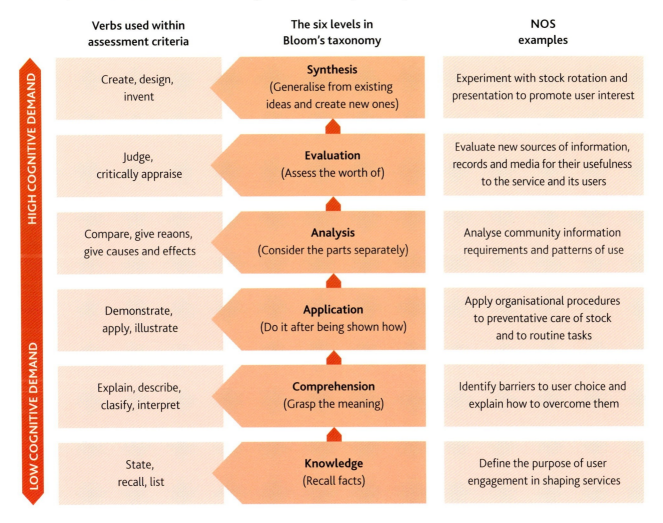

Verbs used within assessment criteria	The six levels in Bloom's taxonomy	NOS examples
Create, design, invent	**Synthesis** (Generalise from existing ideas and create new ones)	Experiment with stock rotation and presentation to promote user interest
Judge, critically appraise	**Evaluation** (Assess the worth of)	Evaluate new sources of information, records and media for their usefulness to the service and its users
Compare, give reaons, give causes and effects	**Analysis** (Consider the parts separately)	Analyse community information requirements and patterns of use
Demonstrate, apply, illustrate	**Application** (Do it after being shown how)	Apply organisational procedures to preventative care of stock and to routine tasks
Explain, describe, clasify, interpret	**Comprehension** (Grasp the meaning)	Identify barriers to user choice and explain how to overcome them
State, recall, list	**Knowledge** (Recall facts)	Define the purpose of user engagement in shaping services

HIGH COGNITIVE DEMAND → LOW COGNITIVE DEMAND

Assessing to 'levels'

Other indicators that may be relevant at initial assessment are those to do with:

• **autonomy:** the extent to which learners must exercise their own judgement and/or perform without guidance or supervision

• **accountability:** the scope and extent of responsibility needed (to complete a task or within a job).

---

[5] From Benjamin S. Bloom et al, *Taxonomy of educational objectives.* (Boston, MA: Allyn and Bacon) Copyright © 1984 Pearson Education. Adapted by permission of the publisher.

QCF level descriptors

Here are two examples of QCF level descriptors at levels 2 and 3 that are used to differentiate between QCF qualifications.[6] Notice how the demand on the learner increases at the higher level.

Level	Summary	Knowledge and understanding	Application and action	Autonomy and accountability
2	Achievement at level 2 reflects the ability to select and use relevant knowledge, ideas, skills and procedures to complete well-defined tasks and address straightforward problems. It includes taking responsibility for completing tasks and procedures and exercising autonomy and judgement, subject to overall direction or guidance.	Use understanding of facts, procedures and ideas to complete well-defined tasks and address straightforward problems Interpret relevant information and ideas Be aware of the types of information that are relevant to the area of study or work	Complete well-defined, generally routine tasks and address straightforward problems Select and use relevant skills and procedures Identify, gather and use relevant information to inform actions Identify how effective actions have been	Take responsibility for completing tasks and procedures Exercise autonomy and judgement, subject to overall direction or guidance
3	Achievement at level 3 reflects the ability to identify and use relevant understanding, methods and skills to complete tasks and address problems that, while well defined, have a measure of complexity. It includes taking responsibility for initiating and completing tasks and procedures as well as exercising autonomy and judgement within limited parameters. It also reflects awareness of different perspectives or approaches within an area of study or work.	Use factual, procedural and theoretical understanding to complete tasks and address problems that, while well defined, may be complex and non-routine Interpret and evaluate relevant information and ideas Be aware of the nature of the area of study or work Have awareness of different perspectives or approaches within the area of study or work	Address problems that, while well defined, may be complex and non-routine Identify, select and use appropriate skills, methods and procedures Use appropriate investigation to inform actions Review how effective methods and actions have been	Take responsibility for initiating and completing tasks and procedures including, where relevant, responsibility for supervising or guiding others Exercise autonomy and judgement within limited parameters

Using detailed descriptors such as these is helpful if, as in apprenticeships, learners are required to achieve a qualification at a particular level. You can use them to compare their entry levels against the level of achievement expected. This helps you to gauge the levels of support a learner will need and their likelihood of success.

If you find that learners are leaving or failing to achieve, it could be that they are finding their programmes either too easy or too challenging. This is because they are learning at the wrong level for them, and you've missed this at the initial assessment stage.

'If you're using RPL, you can't just map or design an evidence matrix from learning achieved at – say – level 2 across to level 3, because this doesn't take account of the increased challenge. You may well be setting the learner up for failure or for a qualification that isn't worth the paper it's written on.'

Assessor

---

[6] *Regulatory arrangements for the Qualifications and Credit Framework*, Annex E (QCA, August 2008)

What the standards say

National occupational standards (NOS) Standard 2:
Identify individual learning and development needs

Knowledge and understanding

KU1 The principles that underpin learning needs analysis for individual learners

KU3 Other requirements from organisations or external agencies that may affect a learning needs analysis

KU4 Methods of reviewing a learner's formal and informal achievements

KU5 Methods of giving recognition for prior learning and achievement

KU6 Methods, which include the appropriate use of technology, to carry out an initial assessment of capability and potential

KU7 How to select initial assessment methods which are safe, reliable and valid for the learner and their objectives

KU10 Who to make agreements with and the issues to consider when prioritising an individual's learning needs

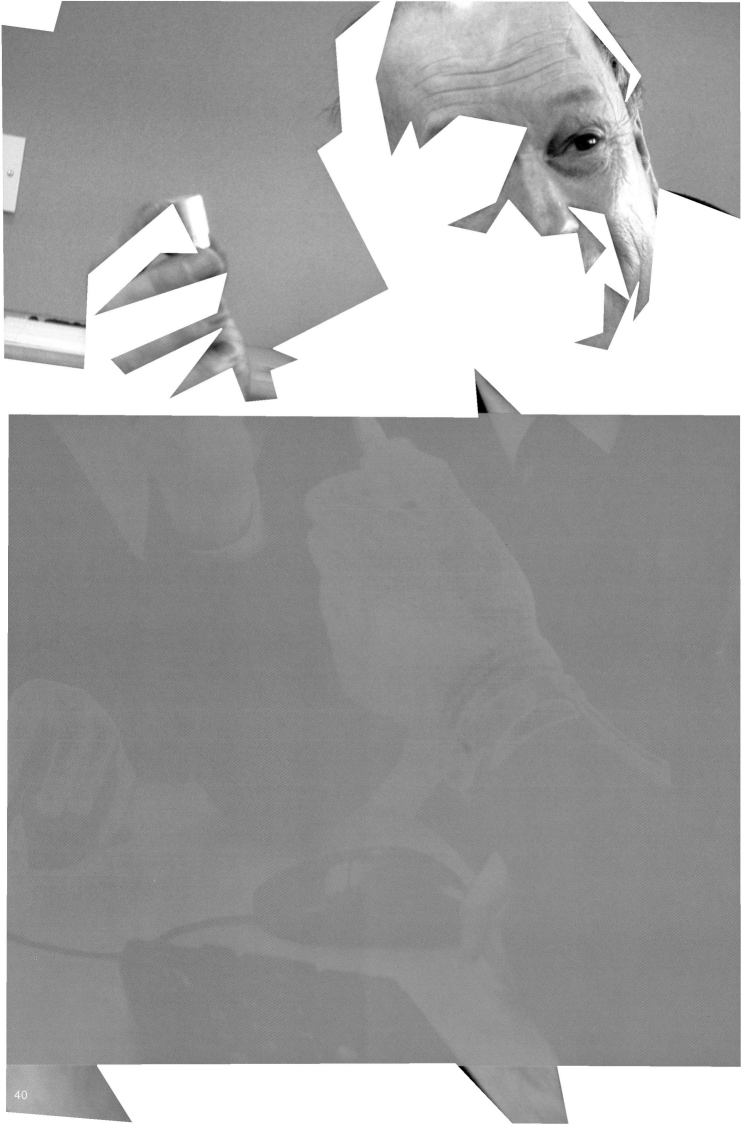

3 Choosing and using initial assessment methods

We can use a wide range of initial assessment activities with learners. We can then use the information gained from these activities in a number of ways, to improve the learners' experience. It's important to understand how to go about choosing the appropriate assessment activity for the circumstances, achieving the right balance between subjective and objective methods.

This chapter tells you when and how to use:

- application forms

- interviews

- psychometric and in-house tests

- self-assessment questionnaires and checklists

- observation of group activities

- previous learning, experience or achievement

  - using documentary sources

  - using RPL

- work tasters.

Subjectivity versus objectivity

Initial assessment can be carried out either objectively or subjectively, or with a mixture of both approaches. You need to use a range of different techniques, to ensure that your IA is accurate and that learners get equal chances and opportunities. This is particularly important if you have a limited number of places on a programme or if you are initially assessing against entry requirements.

You need to make sure that the whole IA process is flexible enough for you to be able to establish each learner's individual needs. At the same time, you should put checks and balances in place to ensure that you are being fair to everyone.

Method	Definition	Example
Objective means...	you get the same results, whoever carries out the assessment.	**Psychometric tests** These tests have strict administration and scoring systems so that any trained administrator will get exactly the same results.
Subjective means...	you get different results, depending upon the experience, personality and/or values of the person carrying out the assessment.	**Interviews** One interviewer may attach more importance to certain information from the interviewee than another interviewer with a different perspective. Proper training can reduce this risk.
A combined approach means...	you use both objective and subjective methods to maximise your strengths and minimise your weaknesses	**Psychometric tests and interviews**

Application forms

Think of the application form as a starting point for other IA methods. Application forms are a good way of gaining basic, personal information about learners and specific information about any accredited learning and qualifications.

As with all the methods you choose, before you collect the information it's important to be clear about how you are going to use it. For example, if you wish to use your application form to identify basic levels of literacy and numeracy, you must tell prospective learners that you intend to do this, so that they have a fair chance of showing you what they can do. However, you will need to back this up with other methods, to confirm their attainment: application forms on their own are an unreliable indicator of attainment or potential.

Strengths and weaknesses of application forms

As an initial assessment method, application forms have the following strengths and weaknesses.

Strengths	Weaknesses
• The same information is requested in the same format from each learner.	• Someone other than the learner may complete the form, or contribute to completing the form.
• They are the most economical method of collecting personal information.	• Some learners are better than others at expressing themselves in writing or online.
• Written or online applications can form the starting point for further exploration at interview.	• Some learners may not pursue an application if they find form filling intimidating.
• They give you time to prepare topics and issues to explore at interview.	• Learners lacking self-confidence may not include information if they perceive it as irrelevant.

What to include in an application form

Here's an example of an application form used with 16–19-year-olds.

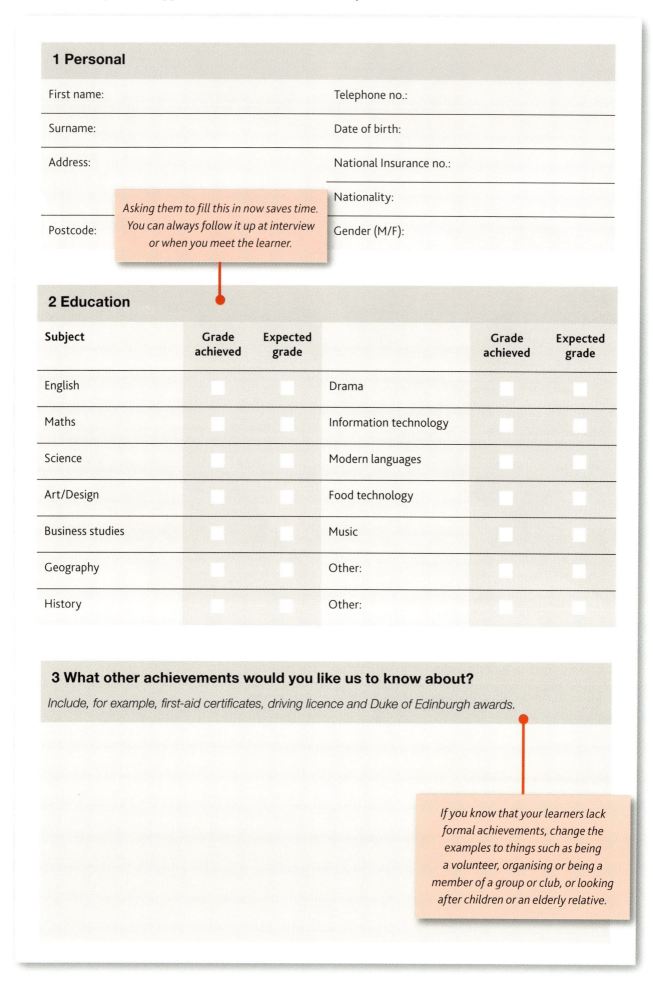

1 Personal

First name: Telephone no.:

Surname: Date of birth:

Address: National Insurance no.:

                                         Nationality:

Postcode: Gender (M/F):

Asking them to fill this in now saves time. You can always follow it up at interview or when you meet the learner.

2 Education

Subject	Grade achieved	Expected grade		Grade achieved	Expected grade
English	☐	☐	Drama	☐	☐
Maths	☐	☐	Information technology	☐	☐
Science	☐	☐	Modern languages	☐	☐
Art/Design	☐	☐	Food technology	☐	☐
Business studies	☐	☐	Music	☐	☐
Geography	☐	☐	Other:	☐	☐
History	☐	☐	Other:	☐	☐

3 What other achievements would you like us to know about?

Include, for example, first-aid certificates, driving licence and Duke of Edinburgh awards.

If you know that your learners lack formal achievements, change the examples to things such as being a volunteer, organising or being a member of a group or club, or looking after children or an elderly relative.

4 Do you have a health issue or disability that we may need to help you with, to enable you to work and/or attend a learning centre?

If they answer yes, follow this up during the interview, once you have established a relationship with your interviewee.

Yes	☐	No	☐

5 What is your ethnic group?

Explain that it's your policy to ask everyone this question.

We ask everyone this question as it helps us to tailor our learning programmes more effectively.

Asian or Asian British – Bangladeshi	☐	White British	☐
Mixed/White and Asian	☐	Black or Black British - Caribbean	☐
Asian or Asian British – Indian	☐	White Irish	☐
Mixed white and Black African	☐	Black or Black British	☐
Asian or Asian British – Pakistani	☐	Any other Black	☐
Mixed white and Black Caribbean	☐	White any other	☐
Asian or Asian British	☐	Chinese	☐
Any other Asian	☐	Any other (write in)	☐
Any other mixed	☐	Prefer not to say	☐
Black or Black British - African	☐		

6 How did you hear about us?

Include a question like this if you want feedback about your recruitment and/or marketing methods.

7 What are your reasons for wanting to join [the name of the learning programme]?

Treat this as a starting point for later discussion, rather than as a way of assessing literacy levels. If you do intend to use this part of the form to screen applicants, say something like: 'We will use your answers to assess your motivation and to choose who we will ask to attend an interview.'

Interviews

Interviews are one of the most commonly used methods of initial assessment, but can be the most unreliable. Few people undergo formal interview skills training, and consequently develop their own ideas about how it should be done. Interviewers may also have favourite questions that they believe enable them to predict certain future behaviours of the person in front of them. Unfortunately, this strategy produces unreliable results and rarely works. With this in mind, it's really important for interviewers and assessors to be trained in formal interviewing skills.

Remember

Think carefully about why you choose to use interviews. If this is your only way of assessing initially, you need to think about including other assessment methods because of the issue of subjectivity.

Strengths and weaknesses of interviews

As an initial assessment method, interviews have the following strengths and weaknesses.

Strengths	Weaknesses
• You can develop rapport with potential learners.	• They can give unreliable results unless well planned.
• You can discuss and explore previous experiences, successes and difficulties and use them to motivate and encourage learners.	• Without training, it's easy to ask ineffective questions.
• You can identify learning support needs.	• The interviewer can make subjective judgements and be prone to bias.

There are three main types of interview:

• structured

• semi-structured

• unstructured or informal.

Structured interviews

A structured interview is one you have planned in advance, with a list of the questions you will ask, and then sticking to your 'script'. Structured interviews are the most useful type to use when recruiting or selecting employees. Using a set procedure for interviews enables all interviewers to ask broadly the same questions of the same types of learner.

Planning interview questions in advance has the advantage of enabling you to review them against equality of opportunity legislation. If you are able to accept only a small number of candidates applying to your employment with training opportunity, you will need to be particularly careful to make sure that your procedure is fair. You must ask similar questions of both females and males, of people from different ethnic backgrounds, and ensure that you are proactive about evaluating and reviewing your procedures (see Chapter 5 for more on equality of opportunity). For example, if you are concerned about childcare in relation to the learners' abilities to attend training or employment, you must ask this of both males and females. Similarly, it would also be unlawful to ask someone from an ethnic minority a question about how they came to be in your area or town if you do not ask everyone the same question.

Semi-structured interviews

This is the most appropriate type for interviewing prospective learners. As with structured interviews, the process involves planning the questions that you will ask of all learners, but it also means that you can explore any relevant issues as they arise. A semi-structured approach also means that you can praise, reward and encourage previous learning, no matter how insignificant it appears, to motivate and persuade learners that they can achieve, and that you will do your best to help them.

Unstructured interviews

Unstructured or informal interviews are appealing because they require little effort or planning. However, don't use them as a method of initial assessment because they are inherently unreliable, prone to interviewer bias and unfair.

Using effective questioning

The way you ask questions will determine the quality and usefulness of the responses. For example, asking a series of closed questions will come across as an interrogation and give limited understanding and knowledge of the learner's needs.

Here are some of the different types of question and how you might use them during an interview:

Type of question	Use when...	Examples
Situational (What if...?)	• you want to find out how a learner would react in a particular situation that they may not yet have experienced	Imagine you are being shouted at by an irate customer. How would you feel? What would you do if you were asked to take over from your supervisor for half an hour?
Competency	• you need information about their experiences or about how much they know and can do	Can you give me an example of when you learnt something through doing the job? When would you do that again?
Closed	• you want to confirm your understanding of a previous answer	Does it bother you when you make a mistake? Do you prefer to learn by having a go at things?
Open	• you want the learner to talk, or you want information	Tell me more about... How did you...? Why did you approach the task in that way?
Probing	• you want to know more about something that the learner has said in response to one of the questions above, so you ask a follow-up question.	How did you find that job? Tell me more about what you did each Saturday in the shop.

Preparing for interviews

The usual rules apply when you are planning and conducting interviews: you need to ensure that you create an environment that will encourage your interviewee to talk about themselves and their strengths and weaknesses. How you do this will depend on your potential learners and the programmes you offer.

Many candidates get anxious about interviews and consequently do not interview very well. To help reduce nerves, let candidates know in advance what the interview will cover and how long it will last, and don't keep them waiting. They are more likely to stay relaxed and focused if you stick to your stated timescales.

Interviews should take place somewhere quiet, clean and confidential. Start the interview with an informal chat to help break the ice, describing the format of the interview, what its purpose is and the kinds of questions you will be asking. Ensure that you have all the relevant documentation from the candidate – such as their CV or application form – to hand.

'We deliberately don't use a formal setting or we'd put our learners off. Many of them have had quite negative experiences of being formally assessed in the past, so we sit down with them in our coffee area and talk to them. However, we use the same interview format and ask the same questions of all our potential learners, so our procedure is fair.'

Training co-ordinator

Activity: Interview preparation

Use the following checklist to help you when preparing for interviews. Aim to answer yes in every case. Space has been left for you to add any items you think are important.

Question	Yes	No
1 Is the furniture suitably arranged? (For example, avoid head-to-head confrontations across a desk, or having your chair higher than the interviewee's.)		
2 Is it a comfortable environment? (Is it warm or cool enough? Are drinks available?)		
3 Have I made sure we will be free from interruptions?		
4 Have I made definite arrangements with the interviewee?		
5 Does the interviewee know what to expect?		
6 Do I know what I want from the interview?		
7 Am I adequately prepared, with the candidate's application to hand, a list of questions to ask and tests ready to go?		
8 Other		

Non-verbal communication

We all communicate in different ways, and the words we use when we talk account for a very small part of our overall message. 'Body language' or, more accurately, non-verbal communication, can communicate up to 70 per cent of what we want to say or mean.

Body language, just like any other language, varies between different cultures and societies. For example, in white British body language, engaging in eye contact is seen as positive, meaning that the person is paying attention and interested. However, in many other cultures, making eye contact is a sign of disrespect or aggression. Trying to 'read' someone's non-verbal communication is a specialist task so, unless you've been formally trained, don't rely on conclusions based on your understanding of body language.

There are four basic positions that you can look out for, however:

- **Open**

Learners facing you with both feet planted on the ground, and showing open hands, are likely to be accepting your message.

- **Closed**

Learners in the closed position, with their arms clasped around the body or folded so that hands do not show, legs crossed or wound around each other, and body or legs turned away from you, may be indicating that they are rejecting your message.

- **Forward**

Forward/back can indicate whether learners are actively or passively reacting to communication. When they are leaning forward, with shoulders slightly rounded and facing towards you, learners are more likely to be actively accepting your message.

- **Back**

Leaning back, playing with or attending to other things (fiddling with hair or pieces of paper, etc.) usually means that the learner's attention is elsewhere. They may be either passively absorbing or ignoring what is being said.

The combinations of open/closed and forward/back can also give you clues about the learner's response:

- open/forward – the learner is likely to be responsive

- open/back – they are likely to be reflecting on what you are saying

- closed/back – they are likely to be feeling they want to escape

- closed/forward – they are likely to be actively resisting.

The easiest way to tell that a person is engaging in the interaction is that they are facing you with their body and feet pointing towards you and 'mirroring' your positions. If their head is facing you but their feet and body are pointing away from you, they may be feeling uncomfortable.

Mirroring is when both people adopt the same position – as it would be if you were looking at each other in a mirror. Mirroring someone's position is a good way to establish a rapport with them as it has a relaxing effect and indicates that you are both thinking similar thoughts.

Assessing motivation

One of the biggest problems in an IA interview is being able to assess a learner's motivation. We often assume that all learners want to be on a particular programme at the beginning, when often the reverse is true. While learners applying for longer-term programmes or higher-level qualifications are usually very motivated and quite happy to go through an initial assessment process, many others are there only under duress. Their parents or a line manager at their workplace may have told them to get on the programme, or they are there simply so that they can collect their benefit.

'We often have to work with learners who don't want to do the training in the first place. They are difficult to engage and certainly don't want to go through an extensive interview or assessment process, no matter how much we explain that it is for their benefit. They just want to get on with the training as quickly as possible! For such learners, we need to find ways of making the IA process meaningful and there is no magic answer to this. For us, the main point of IA and induction is to get to know the learner and establish a rapport with each one.'

Teacher

To find out more about learners' motivation, you need to work with them to explore their reasons for wanting to join a particular programme. In doing so, you are aiming to find out:

- whether or not they want to be there
- whether they are ready to engage actively in learning.

If the answer is yes in both cases, the learner stands a good chance of succeeding. If, on the other hand, the learner answers no, you must face honestly the question of recruiting them or allowing them to continue. Dealing with learners' motivation at this stage will affect your future achievement and retention rates more than anything else. If you avoid the question, be prepared for potential problems such as dropping out or non-attendance at a later stage.

In-depth motivational interviewing involves using a set of principles to explore an individual's preparedness for change, and requires specialist skills. If you plan to explore learners' motivation, you need to have good counselling skills and some formal training in motivational interviewing.

The first interview

Here is a suggested format for carrying out an initial interview with a young learner.

Remember

You will come across learners who appear highly motivated at interview, and yet they are some of the first to drop out. This may be because they are good at interviews and come across well, or they tell you what they think you want to hear, or they may just enjoy the challenge of the interview.

Interview record

1 Setting the scene ●————————————

List some neutral, prompt questions such as: 'How did you get to the interview?' or 'Did you have any difficulty finding us?'

You don't need to record the responses to these initial questions – the important thing is to give your interviewee a chance to relax and focus on the interview itself.

2 The future ●————————————

Have in front of you the learner's educational achievements, such as GCSE results or predicted grades.

What career or job ideas do you have?

What made you choose these?

Would you like to investigate other job or career ideas?   Yes   No

If yes, which ones?

What work experience do you have of the above choices, or any other?

3 Education and achievements

Did you stay at school until the end of year 11?	Yes	No

Did you/are you taking any exams? Tell me about the ones you hope to achieve.

(If the learner left early) Could you tell me why?

(If the interviewee didn't complete school) How did you spend your time?

What did you learn?

For example: how to occupy yourself and not to get bored

What have you done in the last few years that you are proud of or have enjoyed?

Here, you are looking for significant aspects of achievement to build on and use to motivate and encourage the learner to enter learning and to persevere.

Tests

If you are going to use a test or formal assessment as the basis for decisions about appropriate levels of provision, you must be able to establish whether or not it is a quality product before using it. Learners who feel that they have been unfairly placed on an inappropriate course or level because of the initial assessment often have legitimate cause for complaint. The following example is well known in recruitment practice and serves as a warning of what can happen if your initial assessment methods are unfair.

Unfair tests

Some years ago, eight Asian British Rail guards brought a case under the Race Relations Act 1976. Nineteen Asian and six white applicants applied for retraining as drivers. None of the Asian applicants was successful, but four of the six white candidates were. British Rail lost the case. A consultant psychologist successfully argued that those for whom English was not their first language typically scored less well on verbal reasoning and comprehension tasks, and thus the Asian applicants were judged to be disadvantaged when these abilities were involved in timed tests.

Psychometric tests

Psychometric literally means 'mind measurement', from psycho = mind and metric = measurement.

Any test that measures aspects of the mind such as aptitude or personality could be called psychometric. Although tests like these aren't difficult to understand, you must be trained to use them properly. If you know what you're doing, you will find them a valuable objective assessment method in these areas:

- establishing aptitude and potential
- assessing ability and attainment
- exploring personality
- looking at motivation.

The information gained from well-constructed tests can help you match learners to appropriate learning programmes.

Test producers and publishers spend a lot of time and money ensuring that psychometric tests are fair. Fairness can be assured by looking at the qualities of the test. These are:

- reliability
- validity
- standardisation in administration and interpretation.

Reliability

When you use a test or assessment, you need to know that the results are as accurate as possible. No test or assessment will ever be 100-percent accurate, as human beings are unlikely to behave in exactly the same way twice. The key, however, is to reduce the margin of error as much as possible to ensure that the test produces consistent results, as in the following example.

Perfect eggs every time?

Imagine that you are trying to make perfect scrambled eggs. You follow the recipe exactly and use two eggs, a pinch of salt and a tablespoon of milk. You beat up the eggs with a fork, add the salt and milk and beat again. Next, you put a teaspoon of butter in the saucepan and use the middle-sized burner on your hob. You cook the egg for three minutes. On the first occasion you are really pleased with the results and decide to have scrambled eggs again the next day. The next day the result is not as wonderful, even though you followed the recipe exactly as you did the day before. Your scrambled eggs are almost the same, but not exactly.

When assessing the reliability of a test, you want to be sure that you will obtain almost the same results, but not necessarily 'exactly' the same results, whenever you use it. When you are sure about a test's reliability, you can make fair comparisons between learners and fair judgements about progress made.

Validity

Validity is a technical assessment of the test's ability to measure whatever the test producer wants it to measure. For example, if someone wanted to know how well you could drive a car, they would probably get into a car and go for a drive with you – they would be unlikely to ask you to accompany them on a bicycle ride! In other words, there needs to be a good relationship between the topic of the test and what the test is being used for. It seems like common sense, but it can be very tempting to select parts of a test to save time, or use parts of different tests in the hope of producing a better test. Doing this will invalidate the test. In addition, commercial tests are usually protected by copyright legislation, so you would be breaking the law if you did this.

Invalid assessment methods

Many awarding organisations (AOs) use multiple-choice questionnaires (MCQs) to assess what learners know in the cognitive domain. MCQs contain the answer as one of the options within the question itself, so it's a valid method if you want the learner to be able simply to identify the correct answer. However, it is an invalid method to use if you want to see whether the learner can explain something, because it doesn't prompt that kind of response.

Similarly, asking the learner to write an account of what they've been doing is an invalid method to use if you are assessing whether or not they can actually do the task or job they are writing about. This is because applying skills is concerned with the psychomotor rather than the cognitive domain (see Chapter 2). However, asking for a learner account would be valid if you're assessing the ability to describe something.

Standardisation in administration and interpretation

Psychometric tests are standardised. This means that there are prescribed ways of using the test, administering it, and interpreting the results. It is only by following the instructions on administration and interpretation precisely that you can be confident that the results are reliable.

Designing your own tests

Designing your own tests may seem like a cheap option, but it is most unlikely to give you the accurate results you need for good IA. Unless you have the technical expertise to design a sound test – you are a qualified occupational psychologist, for example – this approach is not recommended.

Self-assessment questionnaires, checklists and skillscans

Self-assessment questionnaires, checklists and skillscans are good ways of gathering essential information for initial assessment.

'We only use self-assessment questionnaires as an initial assessment method for candidates taking qualifications at level 3 or beyond. We don't use these for those at level 2 and below. We also use a training needs analysis form to ascertain gaps in knowledge prior to learners undertaking their training with us, as it allows us to gather a lot of information which we need for a more demanding qualification such as those at levels 4 and 5. We also look at the standards with the learner during a pre-initial assessment meeting and work through the learning outcomes and assessment criteria, then use the TNA form to identify how gaps will be addressed by arranging additional support, courses or on-the-job-training as appropriate.'

Trainer

They involve asking the learner direct questions about themselves or their performance. You can use them to:

- identify tasks that learners have done before

- identify relevant experiences that the learner has had

- gauge whether or not learners have access to particular opportunities, such as those necessary to gain a particular vocational qualification

- give learners the opportunity to assess their own strengths, weaknesses and support needs across a range of skills and abilities.

Self-assessments are straightforward to design. The key is to be clear about the areas where you want the learner to self-assess. To make it as easy as possible for the learner, be specific and ask direct questions. For example, here are some questions to ask a learner about their health and safety knowledge and competence.

Do you...	Yes, and I can prove it	I'm not sure	No – I need further help
know about your responsibilities under the HASAW Act?			
know about employers' responsibilities under the HASAW Act?			
know how to conduct a risk assessment?			
know about the different types of fire extinguisher and how to use them?			
keep an accident book?			
know what to do in the event of fire or an emergency?			

Strengths and weaknesses of self-assessment methods

As an initial assessment method, questionnaires and checklists have the following strengths and weaknesses.

Strengths	Weaknesses
They are reasonably easy to construct and use.	Learners who are eager to present a positive self-image may overrate their abilities.
You can gain a great deal of information relatively quickly.	Higher-ability learners' self-reports are more reliable than those of lower-ability learners.
Learners are actively engaged in assessing their own needs.	Females tend to under-report abilities while males tend to over-report abilities.
You can design them to be occupationally specific.	
They are a good starting point for exploring further needs.	

Observation of group activities

Setting group tasks, and observing how learners perform, gives you the opportunity to look at a range of tasks from which inferences can be made about learners' abilities and learning support needs.

Observation lends itself to assessment of learners' ability to:

- communicate and work with others

- follow instructions

- work to deadlines

- solve problems.

Observation requires careful planning and preparation, and you need to be aware of potential pitfalls, such as:

- **unfairness**

As an observer, you will need to be trained to observe as fairly as possible, otherwise you may be unfair without realising it. For example, some learners will attract your attention more than others, and so you will be inclined to notice and judge them more frequently than you will others.

- **'over-focus'**

One way to avoid over-focus is to construct behavioural statements in your observation record, rather than evaluative and subjective ones. For example, 'gets on well with others' means that you are making a subjective, evaluative judgement about the behaviour of a learner. Two observers observing the same piece of action could come to different conclusions because they may disagree about what 'getting on well with others' means. An alternative – and fairer – observation would be a more factual statement such as 'spoke to group as a whole'. This is a statement that can be answered by 'yes' or 'no'. By watching a learner, you can simply count how many times they spoke to the whole group.

Making the most of induction

Review your induction process to see if you are making the most of existing group activities as opportunities for initial assessment. You may find ways of extending such activities or including new ones. For example, induction into an apprenticeship usually requires induction into equality and diversity, as well as health and safety. You can design these sessions to include observations of learners' skills and abilities, thus making the activity more cost- and time-efficient.

When observing more than two people, writing comments is not a reliable recording method. A better alternative is to use the 'five-bar-gate' method. Here, you draw a line each time you observe someone demonstrating a particular behaviour, and then group the lines into fives, as shown on the chart in the example session below. This makes it quicker to interpret the results at the end of the exercise. You will make fewer errors if you use a highlighter to colour each behavioural statement before you start, as you will quickly get to know the statement each colour represents. This will be especially true if you regularly use the same rating grid.

The following example is taken from a session on equality and diversity, where learners' abilities to discuss topics were being initially assessed.

'We used to sit them down and tell them about health and safety. Now we have three or four individual and group activities that they all do. We use this as a way of asking about how they prefer to learn and tackle things. They usually find it easier to work in a small group when answering the quiz questions, so we use this as a way of discussing team-working.'
Trainer

Observing an equality and diversity session

For this activity, one member of staff was needed to run the session and another was required to do the observation, making notes on all the participants.

In this activity, a group of seven learners was shown five photos and asked to discuss them. Their task was to decide what jobs each of the people in the photos did. They were given five job titles and had to allocate them to the photos. In making their choices, the group had to come to a unanimous decision. The purpose of the activity was for learners to realise that you cannot make reliable judgements about people just by looking at them.

Communication skills	Sanvita	Jo	Emma	Yeshim	Devon	Chris	James
Raised a new point	1	1	111		1		11
Spoke to the whole group	1	11	卌 11		1		1111
Made relevant comments	11	1	1		11	11	1111
Appeared to listen	1	111		1	1	1	11
Used positive body language	11	11		1	111	1	11
Summarised group discussion points		1			1		111
Made a decision	1	1	卌		1		11
Spoke to one or two members of the group	1	1		1111	1	11	1

Immediately, you can see, for example, that Emma seemed unable to listen to others' contributions and dominated the activity, while Yeshim was very quiet and reluctant to speak to the whole group.

This five-bar-gate method of recording your observations is not an exact science, but simply a way of structuring the means by which you make judgements about learners. Learners can become angry if they feel they are not being judged fairly, as in the following example.

Unfair judgement

Two 15-year-olds, Becky and Nicola, were doing work experience at the same company in the same office, but for different supervisors. One of the girl's parents took them both to work each morning. At the end of the period, each supervisor was asked to judge attendance as good, average or poor. Becky's timekeeping was judged as good, while Nicola's was judged as average. Both girls arrived at exactly the same time each day and, as a result, Nicola was upset.

You can use observation of group activities in other areas, including:

- health and safety
- learning styles and preferences
- personal learning and thinking skills (PLTS).

Strengths and weaknesses of observation of group activities

As an initial assessment method, observation of group activities has the following strengths and weaknesses.

Strengths	Weaknesses
• It assesses what learners can actually do versus what they say they can do – so it's useful for backing up self-assessment methods.	• It takes time to develop a good observation procedure and recording system.
• It can be economical, for example by using induction activities to gain initial assessment information.	• Observation can be expensive to resource: for example, you need adequate numbers of competent observers.
• It's an opportunity to observe particular individual needs that may not have been seen or assessed elsewhere.	• You may need to develop a range of appropriate tasks or activities. Again, this takes time and resources.
• It's highly effective if there are adequate numbers of competent observers.	
• It's a good way of supporting or confirming other initial assessment information.	
• The more you use the same grid, the more cost-and time-effective it becomes.	

Taking account of previous learning

There are two main reasons for looking at your learner's previous learning as a method of initial assessment:

- to gain a general picture of their current potential in the light of what they have already done

- to gauge whether or not they have evidence that means they can be assessed by going through your RPL process.

General sources of information

For general information about a learner's past learning or achievement, the first and easiest place to look is in their documents. These documents may show evidence of what the learner has done, so talk to them about these. However, learners who have retired or who have been out of mainstream learning or employment for long periods may have little documentary evidence to show what they have done in the past. You need to handle this topic sensitively with them, focusing instead on discussions about other, positive day-to-day experiences of learning.

Several sources of documentary information may help you build up a picture of a learner's general attainments. These are:

- their school progress file (or Record of Achievement)

- recruitment and appraisal information from employers

- their curriculum vitae

- references

- qualifications

- records of training courses attended

- work products or portfolios showing work or projects undertaken.

All these forms of documentary evidence may be useful, but they do have weaknesses, as shown in this table.

Documentary evidence	Useful for...	Weaknesses
Progress file	• providing a comprehensive record of past experiences and achievements	Not all learners have one, or they may not see its usefulness.
Information from employers	• preventing duplication of IA activities, provided you can rely on the quality of the information	Employers may be unwilling to allow access to specific information. You may not gain the whole picture.
Curriculum vitae	• giving you an overview of someone's career and learning	The individual chooses what goes in their CV – and what to leave out.
References	• allowing you to check basic details, such as time spent with a particular employer	Referees are often reluctant to put their true views in writing.
Qualifications	• deciding whether or not it's worth the learner making a claim under your RPL process	There are huge numbers of qualifications: you need to know that the learner can still meet the standards in question if they are making a claim and that you can make a reliable judgement.
Records of training courses	• showing that the learner understands about learning	The content or quality of the course may be unknown, which leads to difficulty in making judgements based on them about what the learner knows or can do.

Assessing using RPL

If your learner wishes to claim credit via RPL, you must assess evidence of their knowledge and performance against the relevant units, learning outcomes and assessment criteria, using assessment methods that are valid and reliable.

There are three kinds of evidence:

• **performance**

This is direct evidence that the learner can still do something.

• **product**

This is concrete evidence of the outcomes of the learner's performance or knowledge; or it could be evidence of previous performance, such as a video or an e-file.

• **knowledge**

This is evidence of what the learner knows.

Remember

RPL is about prior learning and experience – it's not just about qualifications, although they form a useful starting point.

Choosing the right assessment methods

Here are the main assessment methods to use for each type of evidence and the links to learning domains.

Type of evidence	Assessment method	Learning domain
Performance	**Observation** Questioning and/or professional discussion in conjunction with evidence of them having performed the skills/tasks in question Use of others (witness testimony) Simulation (if it's allowed)	Psychomotor (what the learner can do or apply in practice)
Product	**Examination of product evidence** Questioning Professional discussion	Psychomotor Cognitive (what the learner knows)
Knowledge	Questioning (oral and written) Assignments, case studies and projects Discussion Looking at learner statements (reflective journals, for example) Tests (online or paper-based)	Cognitive Affective (values)

For more information on choosing and using assessment methods, see Read, H., *The best assessor's guide* (Read On Publications, 2011).

Work tasters

Using work tasters or work experience is a valuable way of ensuring that learners have a fair idea about what it will be like to work in a particular industry. If you decide to use work tasters as a method of initial assessment, you must first think about how to structure the experience so that you gain the information you need and can make fair or reliable decisions as a result.

Work tasters in dentistry

One training provider recruits and trains dental nurses. As part of the initial assessment and recruitment process, applicants spend one week in the dental surgery. Dental surgeons rate applicants using a set of behaviourally anchored rating scales. These are based on objective criteria, to ensure that there is consistency in the information gained and the judgements made, as different dental surgeons rate the applicants. The process helps the dental surgeons making the judgements to keep subjective opinions to a minimum.

Each prospective learner has a record on which individual grades are recorded. Judgements are made against certain criteria, as follows.

Presentation and appearance	Score				
Hair suitable for surgery hygiene	1	2	3	4	5
Uniform presentation	1	2	3	4	5
Jewellery conforming to surgery requirements	1	2	3	4	5

These criteria are supported by the following behaviourally anchored rating scales:

Hair suitability	
Hair clean, tidy and away from face	5
Hair clean, needs minor adjustment, i.e. tied back	4
Hair clean and of appropriate appearance	3
Hair clean, untidy, needs constant adjustment	2
Hair not clean or in an unprofessional style or colour	1

Uniform presentation	
Clean and smart	5
Clean and ready for work at the start of the day	4
Clean and presentable	3
Not well presented	2
Not clean and tidy	1

Jewellery	
No jewellery	5
Earrings of a sturdy nature	4
Earrings or hair clips	3
Any jewellery other than the above	2
Having been informed of health and safety, still wearing jewellery	1

All applicants are assessed in broadly the same way, reducing problems that occurred previously when dentists based judgements on whether or not they liked the applicant. This method of structuring observation of elements such as presentation and appearance helps to ensure equality of opportunity. You could, however, argue correctly that some of the criteria in the above example are not strictly objective.

Here's an example of objective behaviourally anchored rating scales used to assess timekeeping.

Timekeeping	
Arrived for work before 8.50 a.m.	4
Arrived for work between 8.50 a.m. and 9 a.m.	3
Arrived for work between 9 a.m. and 9.10 a.m.	2
Arrived for work after 9.10 a.m.	1

Using self-assessment in work tasters

Another approach is to structure a self-assessment checklist for the learner to complete. This encourages the learner to take an active part in assessing their own suitability, and encourages them to think more deeply about the implications of going into a particular industry. A useful extension of this technique is to ask prospective employers to complete the same checklist. When both have completed the list, the learner and prospective employer compare the similarities and differences. In this way, any incorrect perceptions of the job and/or their abilities can be discussed.

Here are some examples of statements to use in a self-assessment checklist, where the answers range from 'strongly disagree' (1) to 'strongly agree' (7), with 'neither agree nor disagree' at number 4.

	1	2	3	4	5	6	7
I have a good attendance record							
I adapt well to new situations							
I treat health and safety very seriously							

Choosing the best IA method

The following chart shows you how you could use each assessment method.

	Interviews	Tests	Psychometric tests	Self-assessment questionnaires	Observation	Application forms	Evidence of previous learning, etc.	Work tasters
Basic literacy/numeracy skills	X	X	X	X			X	
Learning preferences	X		X	X	X			
Occupational suitability			X	X				X
Occupational and technical skills and abilities	X	X	X	X	X	X	X	X
Existing skills and knowledge	X		X	X	X	X	X	X
Personal skills	X			X	X			X
Learning support needs	X		X	X	X	X		X
Personal circumstances and other personal support needs	X			X		X		
Health or disability	X					X		

Activity: Choosing an initial assessment system

Test yourself with the following questionnaire to see how well you are able to choose the right IA methods.

1 Which type of interview is likely to be the most effective when interviewing learners?

a	Structured	b	Unstructured	c	Semi-structured

2 Why can reading body language lead you to make incorrect assumptions?

a	Body language is cultural	b	Some people have habits that don't reflect what they are really feeling	c	Sometimes we focus on one aspect of body language and don't seem to see the rest

3 Psychometric tests should be well constructed so that they are reliable. What does this mean?

a	They give exactly the right result 100% of the time	b	They give very similar results most of the time	c	They look professional

4 If you design your own assessments in which you are going to score and make a judgement about an individual, what must you ensure?

a	That they are reliable and valid	b	That they use questions that have been used in other psychometric questionnaires	c	That they look professional

5 In what way can self-assessment checklists be problematic?

a	Learners lacking confidence may underrate their abilities and achievements	b	Learners can complete them quickly	c	They are time-consuming to produce

6 Why do work tasters help to reduce drop-out rates?

a	Learners can have a taste of the reality of doing the job	b	They give employers the opportunity to reject the learner before they start properly	c	Learners can test out travel costs and times of public transport

7 Look at the following list of initial assessment methods. In each case, tick one column and say if you think it is objective, mostly objective, mostly subjective or subjective.

Method	Objective	Mostly objective	Mostly subjective	Subjective
Application forms	a	b	c	d
Interviews	a	b	c	d
Psychometric tests	a	b	c	d
In-house designed tests	a	b	c	d
Self-assessment checklists	a	b	c	d
Observation	a	b	c	d
Evidence of previous learning				
a) using documentary evidence	a	b	c	d
b) using the RPL process	a	b	c	d
Work tasters	a	b	c	d

Test yourself: answers

1b. Semi-structured.

2. All statements are true.

3b. They give very similar results most of the time.

4a. They are reliable and valid.

5a. Learners lacking confidence may underrate their abilities and achievements. Learners can complete them quickly may also be correct if the person administering the checklist does not take sufficient care.

6a: Learners can have a taste of the reality of doing the job. They give employers the opportunity to reject the learner before they start properly may be technically correct but is not to be encouraged; answer c may also be correct but no research supports this.

7.

Application forms: c.

Interviews: c or d.

Psychometric tests: a.

In-house designed tests (if properly constructed): a.

In-house designed tests (if not properly constructed): a, but inaccurate and unfair.

Self-assessment checklists: b.

Observation: b.

Evidence of previous learning using documentary evidence: c.

Evidence of previous learning using the RPL process: a*.

Work tasters: c.

*This is because the assessor's decision is subject to internal and external QA or moderation by others, whose job is to ensure that criteria have been consistently applied.

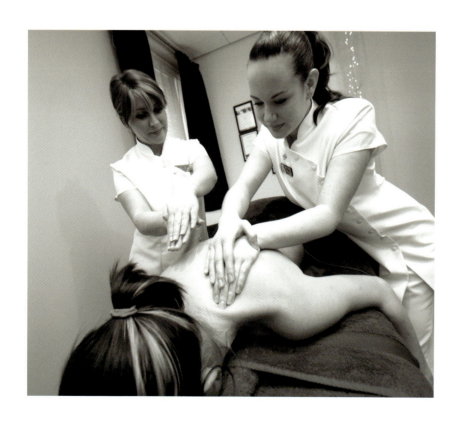

What the standards say

National occupational standards (NOS) Standard 2: *Identify individual learning and development needs*	
Performance criteria	**Knowledge and understanding**
2.1 Identify the learner's objectives, motivation to learn and any requirements relevant to the learning needs analysis	**KU2** Why it is important to identify a learner's objectives and motivation to learn, when analysing their learning needs
2.2 Review the learner's achievements, evaluating these against relevant objectives and requirements	**KU4** Methods of reviewing a learner's formal and informal achievements
2.3 Use safe, reliable and valid methods to assess the learner's capabilities and potential	**KU5** Methods of giving recognition for prior learning and achievement
2.6 Support learners in identifying their own preferred ways of learning	**KU6** Methods, which include the appropriate use of technology, to carry out an initial assessment of capability and potential
	KU7 How to select initial assessment methods which are safe, reliable and valid for the learner and their objectives
	KU11 The communication and personal skills that practitioners need when identifying an individual's learning needs
	KU12 Preferred ways of learning and how these may affect choices about possible learning and development opportunities
	KU13 Different methods of supporting learners to identify their preferred ways of learning, and how to use this information to support their learning
	KU14 Different methods of providing feedback to a learner on the outcomes of the learning needs analysis, and the advantages and disadvantages of these methods

4 Using initial assessment to plan learning

Once you have the results of initial assessment, what do you do with them? The information you have gained should have given you a detailed picture of your learner and their needs, so you can now plan and negotiate with them an effective individual learning programme, or plan.

This section gives detailed advice on how to:

- summarise the outcomes of IA

- give feedback to learners and explain to them what their options are

- help your learners reach decisions

- put together an effective individual learning plan (ILP)

- communicate the ILP to all stakeholders

- link IA results to teaching and learning

- set learning targets and objectives

- choose learning activities

- plan for assessment and review.

What is an individual learning plan?

An individual learning plan (ILP) is a written strategy for each learner that sets personal targets, taking into account the learner's strengths and weaknesses and the way they prefer to learn. It helps the learner keep on track towards where they want to be in their learning programme.

Since the needs of each learner are different, each ILP must be different, since it is tailored specifically to that learner. The learner's role in planning their learning has been shown to be crucial to a productive learning experience, and so, based on the results of initial assessment, the ILP is written after discussion and agreement between the learner and the teacher or trainer.

Summarising the outcomes of IA

The key to effective planning of learning is preparation. Once you have carried out initial assessment, you need to know how to use the information you have gained and turn it into a realistic plan for learning, with input and agreement from the learner. The first thing to do is to summarise the initial assessment information, as in the example on the next page.

Outcomes of initial assessment can give you a profile of the learner's needs – sometimes called a 'spiky profile' because it shows peaks and troughs. The example on page 70 is a spiky profile of one learner's literacy needs.

Using IA to prepare the ILP

At every stage of the process you should involve the learner, by letting them know what you are doing with the information you have gained and inviting them to tell you what they think. As the quote on the right shows, you will save time and effort in the long run by talking through your findings with them and making sure that they understand and agree with the recommendations you put forward. You will need to tailor the way you do this to the individual needs of each learner, taking into account the way they absorb information because this will affect their understanding of what you want to discuss and ultimately influence their 'buy-in' to the ILP itself.

Later in this chapter, you will find different examples of how to use initial assessment to prepare a learning plan, including the way in which one literacy teacher carries out initial assessment and uses the results to inform her teaching.

Key point

An individual learning plan (ILP) is also known as:

- a personal development plan (PDP)

- a personal action plan (PAP)

- an individual training plan (ITP).

Whatever you decide to call it, a learning plan can vary in style and scope. For short courses, it may be completed once and be very brief. For longer learning programmes, the learning plan will be more complex and need to be regularly reviewed.

'You save time in the long run by putting in the legwork at the beginning with the learners. If you do a full initial assessment and explain the results, then each learner is fully prepared for what's to come. When they come to your class, they know that you've got the bigger picture in mind because you've talked it through with them and agreed their needs with them in advance, so you've already gained their trust and co-operation.'

Literacy teacher

Example of an initial assessment summary

Here is an example from an initial assessment for an employed applicant wanting to do an apprenticeship in customer service.

Name: Yolanda Swire		Recruitment adviser: Jeff Swinburn	
What was assessed	**How**	**What was found**	**Recommendations**
Occupational suitability	Self-assessment of access to relevant experience. Interview	Yolanda has been working in CS for 12 months and has access to necessary opportunities	Advanced apprenticeship
Functional English and mathematics	Properly constructed bought-in package	Her current standard is at level 1. She has difficulties with problem solving using calculations	Unlikely to need specific help with written work. Check with assessor after 12 weeks. Needs help with applying mathematical skills. Attend off-the-job sessions.
ICT	Self-assessment questionnaire	Has basic knowledge of Word but does not know how to import images. Uses a spreadsheet package but doesn't know how to do calculations	Needs help with using spreadsheets. Attend off-the-job sessions.
Learning preferences	Self-assessment questionnaire and interview	Enjoys being active and having a go at things. Likes talking to people. Doesn't like sitting in a classroom	Keep off-the-job formal learning sessions to a minimum. Identify someone at work who might be able to mentor Yolanda as she develops her skills
Additional learning/ support needs	Interview	No additional needs identified	
Health and disability	Interview	None disclosed	

Example of a profile of needs

Use a form like this example to capture visually in a 'spiky' profile of needs a learner's performance across several different skills. This provides valuable information about an individual's areas of strength and pinpoints the areas where further learning would be beneficial.

Literacy: Initial assessment results

Name: Richard G

Level	E1	E2	E3	L1	L2
Assessed tasks					
Reading (listening)				X	
Reading (writing)				X	
Spelling			X		
Grammar and punctuation			X		
Speaking and listening (1)				X	
Speaking and listening (2)				X	
Writing task 1			X		
Written composition 2			X		

Giving feedback to the learner

Once you have prepared a summary, the next stage is to feed back this information to your prospective learner and check that they agree with your findings and understand them. It is often said that 'feedback is the breakfast of champions'. Learners cannot be champions if they do not know:

- what they do well already

- what their starting point is

- what they need to do to improve.

At this stage, it may be tempting to sit the learner down and talk 'at' them, and then ask them to sign the ILP. However, time spent here getting learners really involved will motivate them and have a positive impact on your retention and achievement rates.

Structure your feedback and planning session so that the learner remembers as much as possible about what they have agreed to. Think in terms of a three-stage process with a beginning, a middle and an end, as shown in the following table.

The structure of a feedback session

Beginning	Middle	End
• Introduce yourself. • Establish a rapport with your learner. • Explain what is going to happen: i.e. you are both going to discuss the results of the initial assessment activities and then decide on and plan the learning. • Explain the outcomes: there will be a learning plan and they will have a copy.	• This is the main part of the session. Begin by asking the learner how they felt they did in any tests and assessments and teasing out their strong points and areas for further development. • Give them specific feedback on how well they did, and in which areas. Don't hold back – most learners find this the most helpful part of initial assessment, and without it you can't plan ahead. • Explore any issues with them: get them involved in deciding how they are going to build their skills, gain access to relevant experience or improve and develop. • Talk through the options available to them. • Make firm decisions about what will be done, with the learner's agreement. Set targets and objectives and decide how these will be met. • Complete the ILP: ask the learner to do this either in writing or on a PC, which they then print off. Both of you should sign it.	• Restate what has been said and decided. • Check that the learner understands and really agrees (ask check questions). • Complete any documentation. • End positively: 'It sounds to me as if you know where you're going. I think you're really going to make progress and enjoy learning with us.'

Here's how the literacy teacher invites her learners to discuss the results of initial assessment. Notice her friendly tone and straightforward use of language.

Dear Richard

I hope you had a good Christmas and New Year.

Enclosed with this letter are the results of the assessment you did with me before Christmas. The assessment had eight tasks and you will see that you have eight coloured crosses in the results table below. These show how well you did each task and we will use them to plan your learning. They mean the following:

X You are just beginning to develop your skills in this area.

X Your skills are becoming well developed in this area.

X Your skills are already well developed in this area.

The areas in red and yellow are the ones that we need to work on in our lessons to improve your English skills so that you can pass your Level 2 exam.

I think we should concentrate on the areas in red to start with.

I will be talking this through with you during our first meeting, to see whether you agree with me and to give you an opportunity to tell me anything else you would like to do during the course.

I will be seeing Malcolm today to discuss when we are going to start the lessons and will let you know the date by Friday.

Best wishes

Judith

Literacy: Initial assessment results

Name: Richard G

Level	E1	E2	E3	L1	L2
Assessed tasks					
Reading (listening)				X	
Reading (writing)					X
Spelling			X		
Grammar and punctuation				X	
Speaking and listening (1)					X
Speaking and listening (2)				X	
Writing task 1			X		
Written composition 2			X		

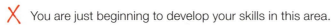

Explaining the options

The next stage is to clarify the learner's options and to get them thinking. Remembering verbal information can sometimes be a challenge, because being told something involves little active thinking on the listener's part. Similarly, if you give learners information to read in long paragraphs of small print on poorly photocopied white paper, they are unlikely to remember very much of it. They are more likely to remember information contained in short, punchy sentences presented as a series of bullet points or as a spiky profile like the one attached to the letter above.

You need to present learning and development options to learners in a variety of ways, for example:

- **verbally:** face to face or recorded orally for those with hearing impairment

- **written:** using simple language, or Braille for those with visual impairment

- **graphically:** using photographs, cartoons and diagrams in a visually stimulating manner, using different colours, shapes or sizes.

'The strength of using the spiky profile is that the learner can see straight away what their gaps are. It's a case of "one picture tells a thousand words" and I know that my learners gained far more from it than me going through the rather wordy results of the IA and how that translated into their ILP. It sat at the front of their portfolios as a visual reminder of how we were working towards "closing the gaps".'

Literacy teacher

Using appropriate language

It is essential to communicate with learners using simple, jargon-free language, whether or not English is their first language.

There are various ways of checking whether you are using language at an appropriate level, including a range of free online tools that will analyse the readability of your text. Search under 'Readability analysis' to find one that includes one or more of the following indicators, then cut and paste your text into the tool for analysis.

- **SMOG (Simple Measure of Gobbledegook) testing** Analysing text using SMOG gives you the approximate reading age needed to read and understand it.

- **Flesch Reading Ease test** Here, the higher the score, the easier a piece of text is to read. A score of 90–100, for example, means that the average 11-year-old can read it. A score of 30 or below means you'd need to be a university graduate to understand it.

- **Collins Cobuild dictionary** This gives you a percentage according to how much a particular word is used. Words with a low percentage are less common and therefore best avoided. More information is available at www.cobuild.collins.co.uk.

You can also use the readability statistics on the 'Tools' menu of your computer.

Helping the learner reach decisions

Learners are far more likely to be committed to their individual learning plan if they make their own decisions about it. Giving learners feedback and realistic information helps them make informed decisions, but you also need to be able to put yourself in their place.

Remember

The planning process means giving learners enough information to enable them to take part and make informed decisions.

As part of the planning process, you need to explain:

- your equality and diversity policy (and safeguarding procedures where applicable) and how this applies to your learner

- your responsibilities under health and safety legislation

- the appeals procedure and how they can use it

- confidentiality: what happens to the information about them and who sees it

- what's expected from them in terms of attendance at learning or training events

- the roles and responsibilities of all those involved in the learning process

- RPL and how this applies.

Your learner may be feeling intimidated, powerless or alienated, or excited, eager and impatient. Their feelings can compromise their decision making, and they may simply go along with a plan because:

- they think you expect it
- they feel they don't have a choice
- they are desperate to change things in their lives and 'move on'
- they think it will please their parents or other people in positions of influence or power.

Getting learners to make decisions involves:

- developing a good rapport with them
- giving learners time to think about or mull over their options and consider the consequences
- listening carefully for hesitations and watching body language
- asking questions about their understanding.

Instead of repeating information, try asking questions instead (without grilling them). Here are some ways in which you can ask instead of telling:

Instead of telling...	Try asking...
You will be coming into the centre on Wednesdays to do functional skills.	Q. What will you be doing when you come into the centre? A. Functional skills. Q. What do you think 'functional skills' are? Etc.
You will have a review with your assessor every 12 weeks.	Q. How often will you be having a review? Q. Who will do a review with you?
The review will involve looking at what you've done and setting targets for what you are going to do over the next three months.	Q. What do you think we'll be talking about during a review?

Putting together an effective ILP

The results of initial assessment tell you about your learners' aspirations, attainments and potential as well as highlighting the areas where they may need help. The purpose of the ILP is to turn this information into a realistic plan, with key targets based on each learner's particular needs and details of their route to achieving them.

The main things to include in the plan are:

1 the overall learning targets and, where appropriate, the specific learning objectives

2 the learning activities (how the targets will be met)

3 assessment and review dates

4 the names of the people involved

5 the resources needed

6 dates and timescales for achieving the targets.

Here is an example of a completed learning plan used by Union Learning Reps (ULRs) working in organisations that are developing the skills of their workforce.

TASTY BISCUITS LTD

Staff development plan

Name: *Peter Green*   Works no. *2379*

Department: Warehouse   Supervisor: *Andy Gibbs*

Internal telephone no. *X 234*   Union Learning Rep: *Rhiannon Jones*

Long-term goal

> Insert a general statement here describing what the individual would like to achieve.

To make the most of my computer at home and be able to send and receive emails from my granddaughter in South Africa

Summary of initial assessment

> Enter headings here for each of the initial assessment activities you carried out, followed by a brief summary of their outcomes.

1. Exploratory discussion/interview

Peter's son has given him a computer so that Peter can email his granddaughter, but his son doesn't have time to show him how to use it.

2. Workplace experience

Peter has not used ICT in his job but other people in his department do, and so Peter feels the skills he will develop will help him at work.

3. Literacy/numeracy

Peter does not have any formal qualifications. He gets by and would be interested in checking out his skills but is not keen to go to a college yet.

4. Information and communication technology skills (ICT)

Has just learnt to turn his own computer on but is apprehensive about having a go in case he gets stuck. He needs help with getting started with ICT.

Learning arrangements

Course title	Where will it take place	Who will monitor progress	Attendance arrangements

Complete this part when the relevant information has been gathered, as agreed in the action plan below.

Action plan

Detail what each person has agreed to do; be as specific as possible.

Action	By whom	By when	Outcome
Find out about suitable basic learndirect courses for computer skills by going to the local learndirect centre in the High Street	Peter	30/08/13	Have a list of courses to choose from
Find out about options to check out literacy and numeracy skills	Rhiannon	30/08/13	List of options

Review arrangements

Include here the frequency of reviews, e.g. 'every 12 weeks'.

Review date	Person responsible	Location
30/08/13	Rhiannon	ULR office

Plan agreed by:

Signed by Employee: *Peter Green*   Signed by Union Learning Rep: *Rhiannon Jones*

Date: *25 May 2013*   Date: *25/5/2013*

Getting the learner involved

The more you involve learners in physically writing and communicating their plans, the more they will be committed to them. You can do this by getting learners to:

- write down or key in their plan in the first instance

- customise or design their own plan

- go through it with their employers and tutors

- comment on their plan and update it as they progress.

Think in terms of helping the learner to think of the plan as theirs and to take ownership of it – this will increase their motivation. However, be honest about what you can allow them to do. It's no good encouraging learners to make their own decisions if you don't have the resources or options available to support them.

Communicating the ILP

Don't record an ILP and then simply file it away; it's just as important to communicate it effectively to all concerned. You need to make sure that not only the learner but also everyone else who's involved in the learner's programme sees and understands the plan.

This means:

- briefing subcontractors, trainers and/or workplace supervisors about individual learners' needs, and involving the learners themselves in this process

- meeting employers and negotiating opportunities for learners to acquire and practise particular skills or tasks, or explaining what's involved in projects or assignments that the learner may be carrying out

- ensuring that the learner has a copy of their ILP and knows exactly what it contains, and why, and when they will carry out the tasks outlined in the plan.

'I ring my learners the day before they start their off-job training, just to make sure they've remembered and that they've thought about how to get there.'
Trainer

'We negotiate learning projects with all our learners and employers. They see it as of benefit to their business.'
Placement officer

Linking IA results to teaching and learning

Here's the literacy teacher's group profile showing how she relates each learner's needs to her teaching.

Literacy: group profile

	Dean	Steve	Richard	Rashid	Dan	Kayne	Carl	Denis	Rob
IA level	1	E3	1	E3	1	1	1	1	E3
Literacy task									
Spelling	Em	C	Em	C	C	C	Em	C	C
Locating info	E	E	E	C	E	E	E	E	E
Grammar (g) and punctuation (p)	C(g) E(p)	E(g) E(p)	E(g) E(p)	C(g) E(p)	C(g) E(p)	C(g) E(p)	C(g) E(p)	C(g) E(p)	C(g) E(p)
Understanding main events, points & details	C	C	C	Em	C	E	C	E	E
Constructing complex sentences	E	C	C	Em	C	C	C	C	Em
Evaluating & comparing info	E	E	E	C	E	C	C	C	C
Punctuating sentences	C	C	C	Em	C	C	C	C	C
Writing composition	C	C	C	Em	C	C	C	C	Em
Using language for different purposes	E	C	E	C	E	E	E	E	C
Sequencing in alphabetical order	E	E	E	E	E	E	E	E	E
Decoding unfamiliar words	C	E	E	C	C	E	E	E	E
Writing in complete sentences	C	E	C	C	E	E	E	E	C
Recognising instructional text language	E	E	E	E	E	E	E	E	C
Recognising different purpose of texts	E	E	E	C	C	E	E	E	C

Teacher's key:

Em = Skills just emerging at this level

C = Skills need consolidation within this level

E = Skills established at this level

Activity: Test yourself

Question	Possible answers	
1 Why is it important to give learners feedback on the results of initial assessment?	a So that they can make informed decisions	☐
	b So that they can tell their parents or employer how well they are doing	☐
2 What's the most effective way to present options to learners?	a Verbally	☐
	b In writing	☐
	c Graphically	☐
	d A mixture of the above	☐
3 Why might learners sign a learning plan when they don't really agree to it?	a They just want to get started	☐
	b They feel they have no other option	☐
	c They want to please you	☐
4 How can learners participate in planning their learning?	a They can write it themselves	☐
	b They can update it themselves	☐
	c They can be responsible for communicating the plan to tutors	☐
5 Using simple language when communicating with learners is important, because most learners have difficulties with literacy.	a True	☐
	b False	☐

Answers: 1a; 2d; 3 & 4: all three are correct; 5b.

Setting learning targets and objectives

Use the SMART acronym to help you set effective targets for learning plans that are:

- **Specific** – they define clearly what is to be done
- **Measurable** – you are able to measure whether or not they have been achieved
- **Achievable** – they are realistic and the learner can achieve them
- **Relevant** – they are worth doing and relevant to the standards
- **Time bound** – the target contains a time limit

The best objectives are always 'SMARTER': they are also Enjoyable and Rewarding.

Here's an example of a SMART learning target:

'To achieve my functional skills in mathematics level 2 by the end of October.'

To achieve a target like this, a learner needs to break it up into smaller, more manageable objectives. This is where initial assessment informs the planning process – the results will tell you the areas in which the learner needs help. Depending on the individual learner's needs, specific learning objectives linked to this target may be:

- to revise percentages using the functional skills worksheets

- to practise using percentages by carrying out the 'costings' assignment between now and July

- to learn how to convert and use fractions and decimals by attending in-house workshops over the next six weeks

- to practise for the test by attending the tests workshop and completing a practice test online in September.

Choosing learning activities

As a training provider, you have access to a variety of activities and resources to help learners achieve their targets. You can link these to the learner's preferred ways of doing things as well as encouraging them to try out new ways of learning. However, you also need to be clear about the limits to learner choice, as the quote on the right illustrates.

While you do need to take account of a learner's preferred learning style, beware of pigeonholing learners according to these preferences. They will benefit from trying out different ways of tackling learning, particularly if you see any mistakes they make as opportunities for learning and give them regular feedback on their progress. You also need to take account of learning opportunities as they arise in the learner's workplace, so be flexible and allow for these when planning with learners.

'In engineering they come straight in to our workshops and do a foundation course. We don't offer them an alternative. This is because the job on the shop floor involves working with machinery, so if this is a problem they probably aren't cut out for the job. We let them try out different ways of working, though. A big part of the job is solving problems, so if they come across one we encourage them to design a solution.'

Group training manager, engineering

Here are some of the main ways in which people learn and some of the activities associated with each one.

If your learner likes to learn by...	You might try...
• doing things	• practical coaching sessions or supervised tasks
• putting ideas straight into practice	• practical assignments or tasks
• working things out for themselves by reading or studying	• self-study materials; online research
• having plenty of guidance or knowing exactly what to do to in advance	• using worksheets, presentations or demonstrations
• non-traditional methods – if they have been put off at school or are returning to learning after a long absence	• e-learning
• experimenting or learning by trial and error	• setting tasks that involve problem solving or letting the learner try things out for themselves
• discussing things with other people	• peer learning or group tasks

'The employer is a fundamental contributor to the process and attends the planning meeting. We try and provide whatever they need, starting with whatever the learner and their employer perceive as a priority.'

Training manager, hospitality

Starting points

It's important to start with the learner's job and plan for training around the needs and skills of the job. However, training providers can still use a range of different starting points. For example, one training manager in hospitality finds out first what training the employee has already received from their company, and then negotiates the ILP around this and their individual needs.

However, it's not just about how the learner prefers to do things. You need to balance this against the resources available, as well as encouraging them to try out different ways of learning.

Planning for assessment and review

Planning learning is not the same as planning for assessment, although you do have to include in the ILP the times when assessment will take place. You need to understand the difference between the two separate processes of assessment planning and reviewing progress, even though you may find yourself carrying them out together.

The purpose of the review process to look at the progress the learner is making and to identify the point at which your learner starts to perform to the standards you intend to assess; otherwise you will waste time and learners will become discouraged.

How the ILP evolves

As learners progress, so their ILPs change accordingly. At the start of the learner's programme, the ILP should show that you have:

- set overall targets and learning objectives to enable learners to acquire the necessary knowledge, skills and attitudes

- set up appropriate learning activities, catering for any special needs the learner may have

- arranged for assessment of prior learning under your RPL process, if applicable (in which case you don't need to plan learning; you can plan for assessment straight away).

In the **medium term**, learners need the opportunity to put into practice what they have learnt until they become confident and competent at what they are doing. At this stage, your job is to:

- modify existing learning objectives and add new ones

- give continual feedback and reinforcement

- take appropriate action in areas where the learner is not making adequate progress

- find opportunities for the learner to put what they have learnt into practice, particularly in the workplace

- recognise the point at which they are performing to standards (national or in-house), as this is when you should plan for summative assessment.

As learners near the **end** of their programmes, you will:

- take urgent action if learners still need help with any aspect of their learning and development

- plan for summative assessment to take place

- arrange for certification.

'You start with the learner's job and link any tasks they do to the optional units of the qualification. These tell you more about the job they do, and you can start to plan for training and assessment from there.'

Assessor

'Our starting point for all learners is 20 weeks in the workshop, learning the basic skills of the trade.'

Trainer, wood occupations

'Until recently, our planning process was driven by the assessment process. We need to focus more on learning and development – how the learner is actually going to learn the knowledge, skills and attitudes they need in the early stages of their programmes. We plan to introduce PLTS learning right at the start of all programmes, because we know they underpin and can help learners acquire the vocational skills, once we've made the links.'

Training manager

Key point

For funding purposes, you may be required to fill in an ILP form at the start of learners' programmes. The examples here are based on practice.

Activity: *Is the ILP good enough?*

Once you have drawn up an ILP with a learner, you may find it helpful to ask yourself the following check questions. Aim to answer yes in each case. Where you answer no, you will need to take action or alter the ILP accordingly.

Item	Check question	Yes	No
The programme	Is the learner on the right programme?	☐	☐
Qualifications	Are the qualifications achievable?	☐	☐
The overall targets	Are the targets based on the results of initial assessment?	☐	☐
	Are they realistic and achievable?	☐	☐
Learning objectives	Are the objectives SMART?	☐	☐
The activities	Are the activities suitable for this learner?	☐	☐
	Are they structured?	☐	☐
	Do they allow for learning to take place? (For example, does the learner have time to learn and apply what they have learnt before producing evidence for assessment?)	☐	☐
	Do the activities take account of opportunities for learning in the workplace?	☐	☐
	Are they relevant?	☐	☐
	Do my learners agree that they are relevant?	☐	☐
Timescales	Are the timescales realistic?	☐	☐
	Do they take account of particular circumstances, such as seasonal changes in the workplace?	☐	☐
Involving the learner	Have I taken account of the learner's individual needs and preferences?	☐	☐
	Do I have proof that the learner is *actively* involved in their own learning (other than a signature)?	☐	☐
Involving others	Does everyone involved know about the results of initial assessment?	☐	☐
	Have I communicated with subcontractors over the provision of any off-job training?	☐	☐
	Is the learner's employer supporting any work-based learning?	☐	☐
	Does everyone else involved know what's expected?	☐	☐

What the standards say

Performance criteria	Knowledge and understanding
2.1 Identify the learner's objectives, motivation to learn and any requirements relevant to the learning needs analysis	**KU2** Why it is important to identify a learner's objectives and motivation to learn when analysing their learning needs
2.5 Agree and prioritise the learner's learning needs	**KU7** How to select initial assessment methods which are safe, reliable and valid for the learner and their objectives
2.7 Give the learner constructive and realistic feedback on their expectations and possible learning and development opportunities	**KU8** How to assess and manage risk when carrying out initial assessments
	KU14 Different methods of providing feedback to a learner on the outcomes of the learning needs analysis, and the advantages and disadvantages of these methods

5 Keeping it legal

You need to ensure that you act ethically with learners and that your initial assessment activities and learning plans comply with current legislation.

The main areas of legislation that apply to initial assessment are those about promoting equality and diversity, people's human rights, protecting vulnerable groups and the use of information. Specifically, the acts are:

- The Equality Act 2010

- The Human Rights Act 1998

- The Safeguarding Vulnerable Groups Act 2006

- The Data Protection Act 1998.

This chapter outlines the principles behind the legislation and what the laws mean for you in your work. Using this information will help you take stock of your current practice and identify possible areas for action.

Equality and diversity

Equality is about creating a fairer society, in which everyone can participate and has an equal opportunity to fulfil their potential. Diversity, meaning difference, is about recognising and placing a positive value on group and individual differences. It means treating people as individuals, so that everyone's needs are understood and responded to appropriately.

The Equality Act 2010 requires equal treatment in access to employment as well as private and public services, regardless of age, disability, gender reassignment, marriage and civil partnership, race, religion or belief, sex, and sexual orientation. In the case of disability, employers and service providers are under a duty to make reasonable adjustments to their workplaces to overcome barriers experienced by disabled people. With limited exceptions, the Act does not apply to Northern Ireland.

It is no longer enough to say you have procedures in place; you now have a general duty to promote equality in everything you do. In practice, this means that you and your organisation must actively challenge prejudice and discrimination, so as to avoid it before it occurs. You also have a legal duty to encourage diversity in all areas – including recruitment into learning programmes of which initial assessment forms an integral part – by treating everyone fairly and creating an inclusive culture for all learners and staff.

Sex discrimination

When the Sex Discrimination Act 1975 was originally passed, it was designed to protect females, but now the law applies to either sex. The legislation has also since been extended to offer transsexuals protection from discrimination on the grounds of gender, both in employment and in vocational training.

What you need to know

1　The Equality Act applies to all sex discrimination in the workplace, such as selection for a job, training, promotion, terms of employment, work practices, dismissal or any other disadvantage such as sexual harassment.

2　Responsibility for sex discrimination usually lies with the employer, but if an employee or worker is found to have discriminated, then the employer will be 'vicariously' liable for them as well. You or your organisation may not intend to discriminate, but this is not regarded as justification should you be taken to a tribunal.

3　The law recognises two kinds of sex discrimination, direct and indirect:

- **Direct sex discrimination** is where a person of one sex is treated less favourably on grounds of sex than someone of the other sex would have been treated in the same circumstances. An example might be using different terms and conditions for the same or similar standard of job.

- **Indirect sex discrimination** can occur where a requirement or condition is applied equally to men and women, but the proportion of one sex that can comply with the condition is much smaller than the proportion of the other sex. Unless it can be proven that the condition is essential for the job,

Key point

The Equality Act 2010 replaced the previous acts and regulations that formed the basis of anti-discrimination law in Great Britain. These included the Equal Pay Act 1970, the Sex Discrimination Act 1975, the Race Relations Act 1976, the Disability Discrimination Act 2005 and the Special Educational Needs and Disability Act 2001. The new act also replaced the three major statutory instruments protecting against discrimination in employment on grounds of religion or belief, sexual orientation and age.

indirect discrimination may have taken place. It has also been established that discrimination against part-time workers may constitute indirect discrimination against women because most part-time workers are women.

What this means in practice

When planning and carrying out initial assessment, you need to ensure that the policies, procedures and language you use are fair to both genders. For example, you must:

- ask the same or similar questions of both males and females

- not use learning materials, tests or assessments that unfairly disadvantage one group

- check that your entry requirements – and those of your employers or subcontractors – do not require skills, qualifications or knowledge that may disadvantage one gender over another. For example, boys are more likely to have an ICT GCSE than girls.

Racial discrimination

The Equality Act requires organisations to promote racial equality and seek to avoid discrimination before it occurs. The aim is to make race equality a central part of the way we all work, by putting it at the centre of policy-making, service delivery, regulation and enforcement, and employment practice. The laws protect everyone from racial discrimination at every stage of employment, including training (and, by implication, initial assessment). The law also explicitly includes all public authorities, and this may apply to you if your organisation is in receipt of government funding.

What you need to know

1 Racial discrimination is outlawed within all public authorities and any functions of these authorities run by the private sector.

2 Public bodies have a general duty to promote race equality and to promote equality of opportunity and good relations between people of different racial groups.

3 Each organisation must have a publicly stated policy on race equality.

4 Organisations must monitor their workforce and take steps to ensure that ethnic minorities are treated fairly. This means:

- assessing the impact of programmes and policies on ethnic minorities

- taking action in areas where there is potential for adverse effects.

5 Bodies must monitor the implementation of policies and programmes to ensure that they meet the needs of ethnic minorities.

6 They must also ethnically monitor staff in all aspects of employment (including analysing grievances, dismissals and other reasons for staff leaving).

7 Public bodies covered by the Act must publish the results of their ethnic monitoring each year.

8 As with sex discrimination, you need to be aware of both direct and indirect discrimination:

- **Direct racial discrimination** is where you treat someone less favourably because of his or her race, colour, nationality or ethnic origin.

- **Indirect racial discrimination** includes using procedures or resources that may seem to apply to all, but actually discriminate against certain groups. This may happen in subtle ways. For example, giving out information only in English may be seen as indirect discrimination. Another example might be if your organisation insisted on a dress code that certain groups could not comply with for religious reasons.

What this means in practice

To comply with the law when carrying out initial assessment, you must:

- take account of cultural differences during face-to-face interviews – for example, by providing access to interpreters and using appropriate body language (see Chapter 3)

- ensure that your assessment methods – such as self-assessments and tests – do not disadvantage one group over another because of the way they are designed, administered or scored

- review all tests, assessments, documents and interviews to make sure the language used is neutral and bias-free – for example, by not using colloquialisms or assuming that learners have local knowledge.

Discrimination on grounds of disability

The law gives equal rights to those with disabilities in areas of employment and access to goods, services, facilities and buying or renting land or property. In education and training, this applies to admissions procedures as well as to access to leisure facilities and accommodation.

What you need to know

1   The Act describes disability as 'a physical or mental impairment which has a substantial and long-term effect on a person's ability to carry out normal day-to-day activities. The disability is to have lasted or be likely to last 12 months or more. If a person has had a disability within this definition, they are protected from discrimination even if they are no longer disabled.'

2   To qualify for protection from discrimination, a disabled person does not have to show that their impairment affects a particular 'capacity', such as mobility or speech, hearing or eyesight.

3   Organisations have a legal duty to be anticipatory, that is, to make adjustments so that people with disabilities can access services where it is reasonable for the service provider to make these adjustments.

What this means in practice

To comply with the law when carrying out initial assessment, you must:

- make reasonable adjustments to the tests or assessments you use, so that they are accessible by someone with a disability, such as a visual or hearing impairment

- ensure that each learning plan is based on a learner's *individual* needs, rather than designed around what is available.

Human rights

Article 8 of the Human Rights Act 1998 concerns the right to respect for private and family life. It means that everyone has the right to respect for their private life, their family life, their home and their correspondence. Public authorities can interfere with this right only 'for the protection of health or morals, or for the protection of the rights and freedoms of others'.

What you need to know

The law's purpose is to balance the rights of individuals with the rights and freedoms of others. Public authorities can justify their exemption to Article 8 in certain circumstances, whereas a private individual or company cannot. If you are not a public body, you may not be an exception under the law.

What this means in practice

When gathering information for initial assessment, you need to:

- make clear your reasons for asking for personal or sensitive information

- make sure that, if you ask for health information, it is in order to protect the health of the individual or that of other trainees/employees.

Safeguarding

The Safeguarding Vulnerable Groups Act 2006 applies to you if you are involved in initial assessment of children and vulnerable adults. The definition of a vulnerable adult is quite wide, and includes anyone over 18, if they:

- are in residential accommodation or sheltered housing

- receive domiciliary care or any form of healthcare

- are detained in lawful custody

- are under the supervision of the courts

- receive welfare service of a prescribed description

- receive payments under the Health & Social Care Act 2001

- require assistance in the conduct of their own affairs.

The Act contains provision for the vetting and barring of individuals wishing to work with these groups. It contains specific requirements for them to register with the Independent Safeguarding Authority (ISA) and for checks to be carried out by the Disclosure and Barring Service (DBS), which replaced the Criminal Records Bureau (CRB) in December 2012.

What you need to know

1   The Act defines two types of activity, regulated and controlled:

- **Regulated** activities cover frontline activities, where people have frequent, direct contact with children or vulnerable adults in health, care or education.

- **Controlled** activities are those that fall outside regulated activities, but which involve contact with children or vulnerable adults and/or access to sensitive information concerning them.

2   It is a criminal offence for employers:

- to employ someone in either a controlled or a regulated activity without checking their ISA and DBS status.

- to allow a barred or unregistered person to work in a regulated activity.

3   Employees' responsibilities under the Act are as follows:

- A barred individual must not take part in any regulated activity.

- A person taking part in a regulated activity must be registered with the ISA.

4   A barred person can work in a controlled activity under certain circumstances, as long as safeguards are in place.

Writing a safeguarding policy

On the next page is an extract from one training provider's safeguarding policy, including what learners are told. This is not intended to be a comprehensive policy that will apply to every organisation. You can use it as a template, but you will need to adapt it and add to it according to your particular learners' needs.

Supporting and safeguarding our learners

At The Best Training Provider we take responsibility for promoting the welfare of all our staff and learners. In the case of children, young people and vulnerable adults, we are proactive in ensuring that we have procedures in place to protect the welfare of these groups and actively promote their sense of wellbeing, including:

- protecting learners from any form of bullying or harassment, physical or verbal, in relation to each area of our equality and diversity policy

- measuring and monitoring our performance in the areas of equality and diversity and linking these to our safeguarding procedures, with the aim of continually improving our performance in these areas

- raising each member of staff's awareness of the need to safeguard young people and vulnerable adults, and of their responsibility to identify and report all signs of possible harm or abuse

- establishing close links with local agencies.

Add agency names such as the police or social services here.

We recognise that a young person or vulnerable adult who may have witnessed or undergone abuse may be unable to maintain a sense of self-worth; and that they may exhibit aggressive behaviour, either in the form of self-harm or towards other people. We accept that the behaviour of learners may range from what is perceived to be normal, to outward aggression or withdrawal. We make it our policy to have trained staff on hand to deal with such behaviour and to encourage and promote a learning environment that is supportive and secure.

You may want to add something here about the disciplinary procedures that will be invoked if a staff member fails in their duty of care.

For our learners: Your safety and wellbeing

We take your wellbeing very seriously while you are training with us.

1. We will make sure that your programme is enjoyable and challenging, and that it meets your individual needs.

2. We will make sure you are safe if there is a fire, an accident or an emergency.

3. We will stop all forms of bullying and harassment – verbal or physical.

This part of the policy is given out and explained to learners at induction.

We will do this by:

- making sure you know who to talk to when you're on our premises. This person is

- asking you about your learning needs and listening to any concerns you may have

- showing you what to do if there's a fire, an accident or an emergency

- asking you about any medical conditions or circumstances that are relevant to you and keeping these confidential, as long as they do not affect the safety of others

- having staff who are trained first-aiders, and who are alert to any signs of bullying or abuse

- telling you about all our procedures during your induction week with us and reminding you about them from time to time

- giving you contact details of the local Children and Young People's Information Service so that, if something happens and we can't help, you can speak to them

- asking you how we're doing: your tutor will ask you questions or you can give us your answers anonymously, if you prefer.

Add the name and contact details here.

Add details here, such as regular fire drills.

Add contact details here.

If you need this document in a different format or you want someone to go through it with you again, just ask.

Say here what you mean by different format, as this will depend on the needs of your learners. For example, it could be a sound file or a document either in larger type or translated into a different language.

Data protection

The Data Protection Act 1998 is the law that regulates processing and storage of personal information relating to individuals, including the ways in which this information is used or disclosed.

What you need to know

The Act covers all personal information, held electronically or otherwise.

- Any organisations holding personal data electronically must register with the Data Protection Registrar, whose job is to enforce the Act.

- When they register, organisations must specify the purpose for which they intend to use the data, which must be obtained lawfully and fairly.

- Individuals have the right to know what information is held about them and to ask to see it.

- If information is wrong, the organisation responsible must ensure that it is amended or deleted.

- Information cannot be given to anyone (companies or individuals) who isn't entitled to it, and it must be protected against unauthorised access, alteration, deletion or disclosure.

What this means in practice

All the information you obtain about your learners is covered by the Act, including information you input electronically, such as:

- individual assessment and/or learning plans

- action plans

- application forms

- results of initial assessment, such as test scores and decisions

- emails containing personal information about specific learners.

To comply with the Act, take account of the following:

1 You and whoever else decides how and why personal data are processed (the Act calls these 'data controllers') need to be open about how you use those data and to comply with data protection principles in your information-handling practices.

2 Your learners have the right to see – and have a copy – of all the information that your organisation holds about them. You must tell them:

- what the information you collect will be used for

- who will process it

- who it will be passed to.

3 Your learners have a right to object to you processing personal data concerning them.

4 You only keep information for as long as is strictly necessary.

5 You must seek learners' permission before you pass on any information to a third party. This includes employers, tutors and anyone else involved in the learning process.

Example of a data protection statement

Here is how one organisation has met the requirements of the Data Protection Act.

The Best Training Provider

Data Protection Statement

So that your training programme can be designed for you as individually as possible, we need to collect some information about you. We may use a range of methods to do this and we have listed these on the chart below. When we have collected this information, our staff, including the tutors, will have access to it. In addition, various statutory* bodies will be able to see it. These include the FE College in Nearbysville, which will be contributing to the funding of your programme, and Ofsted, which may inspect the quality of the learning programme that you are receiving.

In order to comply with the Data Protection Act 1998, we need your permission to share the information that you give us with appropriate bodies. Please sign against each of the items below to confirm that you agree to the information being seen.

Information source	Signed	Date
Interview records		
Online Skill-builder test scores		
Reviews (two-monthy)		
Summative assessments (ongoing)		
Observation notes of personal and social skills activities		
Individual learning plan (ILP)		

You are entitled to see the personal information that we hold about you. Please ask us, at any time, to see your personal records. We may need seven days' notice to prepare them.

We will not pass any personal information to anyone else unless we have your permission to do so.

Signed: Date

Manager, The Best Training Provider

* A statutory body is an organisation that has been established by statute (law) and has the full backing of Parliament.

Activity: *Do we comply with the legislation?*

Use your answers to the following questions to help you identify areas where
you may need to take action. Only tick yes if you can prove that it is happening
in practice.

Area of compliance	Yes, and we can prove it	Not sure	No
Do we collect data on our recruitment and IA policies and procedures that inform our equality and diversity policy?	☐	☐	☐
Are we anticipatory in relation to equality and diversity?	☐	☐	☐
Can we show that our IA procedures and practices enable us to operate within the law in relation to:			
• gender?	☐	☐	☐
• racial discrimination?	☐	☐	☐
• disability?	☐	☐	☐
• sexual orientation?	☐	☐	☐
• religion?	☐	☐	☐
• other? State here	☐	☐	☐
• other? State here	☐	☐	☐
Do we respect all learners' rights to privacy?	☐	☐	☐
If relevant, do all those involved in recruitment and IA comply with safeguarding legislation?	☐	☐	☐
Do we have a data protection policy – and do our learners know about it?	☐	☐	☐
Do learners know what information we hold about them and who sees it?	☐	☐	☐
Have we obtained learners' permission to hold and use all information, including the results of initial assessment?	☐	☐	☐

You are aiming to answer yes in all cases. Where you have ticked not sure or no,
you must take action to ensure that you comply with the legislation in these areas.

What the standards say

National occupational standards (NOS) Standard 2: *Identify individual learning and development needs*	
Performance criteria	**Knowledge and understanding**
2.8 Maintain agreements about confidentiality	**KU15** Why confidentiality is important when identifying learning needs and what information to safeguard

6 Making the business case for IA

There are many ways of establishing a robust IA system, or improving the system you already have. If you are able to establish its costs and relate them to its benefits, you can make the business case to managers for introducing a formal and efficient IA system. You need to 'think smart' about initial assessment from an organisational standpoint, emphasising the fact that a process that capitalises on common pathways and cohorts will not only save your organisation money but also enable it to recruit learners to the programme that meets their needs – and to keep them.

This chapter offers advice on how to make the business case for IA to your organisation. It gives you information on:

- looking at IA and the Common Inspection Framework

- linking IA to your organisation's quality assurance (QA) procedures

- establishing starting points

- gathering information

- using the information you gain to make the case for change.

Initial assessment and inspection

Ideally, initial assessment should form part of your organisation's overall quality assurance framework. If you offer government-funded learning, you will be inspected in the areas of teaching, learning and assessment under the Common Inspection Framework.[7] Since initial assessment is one of the first processes learners undergo, it sets the tone for what is to follow. It underpins the inspection points below.

Quality of teaching, learning and assessment

'[Ofsted] Inspectors will make a judgement on the quality of teaching, learning and assessment by evaluating the extent to which:

- learners benefit from high expectations, engagement, care, support and motivation from staff

  IA should tell you learners' levels of motivation and support needs.

- staff use their skills and expertise to plan and deliver teaching, learning and challenging tasks, and build on and extend learning for all learners

  IA is the starting point for planning learning.

- learners understand how to improve as a result of frequent, detailed and accurate feedback from staff following assessment of their learning

  Learners will gain important feedback as a result of initial assessment at the start of their programmes.

- teaching and learning develop English, mathematics and functional skills, and support the achievement of learning goals and career aims

  Assessment of these skills and aims forms part of IA.

- appropriate and timely information, advice and guidance supports learning effectively

  … and particularly as a result of initial assessment.

- equality and diversity are promoted through teaching and learning.'

  … and are promoted at recruitment and embodied in IA instruments and processes.

---

[7] *Common Inspection Framework for further education and skills* (Ofsted, June, 2012, No. 120062)

IA and the quality assurance cycle

Use your organisation's quality assurance (QA) cycle to help you collect information about its current practice in initial assessment. You can then use this information to make the business case for introducing more formal IA procedures or making improvements to your existing process.

It's important to look at the impact of any IA procedures, because this will tell you whether or not your current procedures are working. This means gathering feedback from learners and everyone else involved in their programmes. Identifying areas for improvement or development will show you where you need to make further changes.

The QA cycle looks like this:

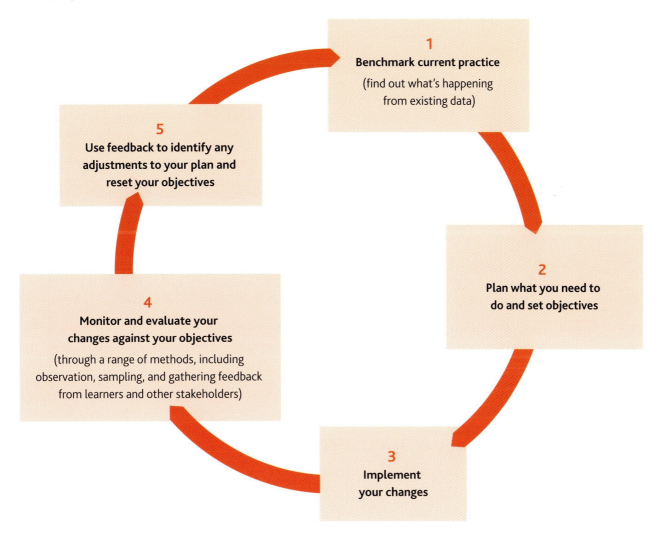

1
Benchmark current practice
(find out what's happening from existing data)

2
Plan what you need to do and set objectives

3
Implement your changes

4
Monitor and evaluate your changes against your objectives
(through a range of methods, including observation, sampling, and gathering feedback from learners and other stakeholders)

5
Use feedback to identify any adjustments to your plan and reset your objectives

Keep going round the cycle as you plan, collect information and monitor, evaluate and reset your objectives as a result. In this way, you will improve your initial assessment system continually over time.

Your starting point: gathering data

To make a business case for change, you will need to gather hard data to show what's happening (or not, as the case may be). Use this data to gauge what this is costing your organisation in terms of lost revenue, funding, people or resource, and then make some recommendations for what should happen.

The following table lists some possible sources of data, with specific suggestions for what to look at and the reasons why you should do so. The issues are all linked to initial assessment and/or recruitment processes.

Data source	Have a closer look at...	Rationale
Retention rates	1 Leaver rates linked to particular programmes 2 The point at which learners leave	Learners may be on the wrong programme. If you find that they're leaving early, it's likely that your IA procedures are inadequate. Those involved in recruitment and IA might lack knowledge or skills.
Achievement rates	1 Learners' starting points compared with levels of achievement expected of them at the end 2 Entry requirements – whether you need to change them, do away with them, or introduce them 3 What your assessors have to say	Learners may be being recruited to programmes that are too demanding for them. If you don't know what learners' starting points are as a result of IA, you won't be targeting their subsequent learning efficiently. Assessors will be able to tell you what's happening when they assess summatively. (However, if you leave assessment until this stage in the learning journey, it may be too late to do anything for the learners.)
Complaints, referrals, appeals	What individual employers/learners have to say	Comparing data from various sources will tell you whether there are common problems in your IA and recruitment procedures – or lack of them.

Continuous quality improvement

When looking at ongoing improvements to the quality of initial assessment procedures, consider using the following methods:

- Observe staff carrying out key initial assessment and planning activities.
- Check how initial assessment tests and assessments are used and interpreted.
- Find out who sees the results of IA and how – or whether – they are acted on.
- Gather feedback from learners, employers and trainers.
- Sample initial learning plans across programmes and cohorts.

Findings taken from a wide range of sources will give you solid evidence that will help you identify specific areas that need improvement.

You may wish to look at the following four areas in more detail.

'I already had the three-unit QCF assessor qualification when I joined an initial teacher training course. One of the assessor units also forms an optional unit of this qualification, but I was not offered credit transfer and had to do the whole course, including an assignment on assessment. I found out later that the tutor wasn't aware that you could do this.'

Learner

1 Observing what happens in practice

Initial assessment activities that lend themselves to observation include:

- interviews
- how initial assessment tests are administered
- feedback given to learners
- information, advice and guidance (IAG) given to learners
- negotiating learning plans with learners.

Often, though, you just need to find out what's happening and whether or not basic communications are taking place, as the quote on the right illustrates.

2 Sampling

Sampling means looking in more depth at a representative selection of assessments or plans. You might consider sampling the scoring and interpretation of the tests or assessments you use and the quality of individual learning plans.

Here are some questions to ask yourself:

- Are we scoring and interpreting the results of tests and assessments correctly, according to the instructions?
- Are the decisions we are making based on the results of initial assessment? Are they consistent among different members of staff and/or different occupational or curriculum areas?
- Are we recording the results of initial assessment consistently, and are all learners getting the same or broadly similar access to support from the outset?

3 Gathering feedback

This is where you actively seek feedback from learners, tutors, employers and any others involved in the process. Do this by using formal methods such as questionnaires or follow-up telephone interviews.

'When I was first appointed, I realised – to my horror – that we were making learners carry out all these tests and that none of our teachers received the results, let alone acted on them!'

IA Co-ordinator

'I sent co-ordinators in to observe how tests were being administered in each of our centres, and I realised our procedures were inconsistent and unfair to learners. Some trainers were letting learners take as much time as they needed and letting them talk and use their phones, while others were giving them a time limit and taking their phones away.'

Training co-ordinator

QA at Uppercut Academy

Quality assurance is an integral part of initial assessment procedures at Uppercut Salons. Here, trainers take a team approach to identifying and making changes.

Two or three weeks after their initial assessment, learners are sent a questionnaire asking for their opinions of the process. On one occasion, when their responses were analysed, it became clear that learners were unhappy with the interviewing process. Many said they weren't given enough time to speak, so staff decided to change the way they conducted the interviews. As the training manager put it:

'We basically stopped explaining and doing all the talking, and instead asked them what they expected from us. It's worked: learners prefer it this way, and we also collect a lot more information about them.'

4 Making comparisons

If you decide to make changes, it's a good idea to plan to have 'before and after' comparisons, using key performance indicators such as learner retention and achievement rates. Depending on the extent of the changes you think will be necessary, you can make comparisons of the whole process or concentrate on just one or two areas where you know that there are already problems.

Activity: Are we following best practice in IA?

Answer the questions below honestly.

Do we...	Yes	No
• include IA and recruitment as part of our QA?		
• know what happens to the results of IA and how they are acted on?		
• know if our IA procedures are working?		
• observe good practice in:		
• interviewing?		
• test administration?		
• IAG?		
• negotiating ILPs?		
• sample test conditions and assessment results?		
• obtain feedback about our IA procedures from:		
• learners?		
• employers?		
• trainers?		
• other key people?		

You are aiming to answer yes in every case. Where you have answered no, you may need to take action.

What the standards say

National occupational standards (NOS) Standard 2:
Identify individual learning and development needs

Knowledge and understanding

KU8 How to assess and manage risk when carrying out initial assessment

Also available from Read On Publications

The best assessor's guide

A guide to best practice for assessors.

It contains

- links to the assessor qualifications and the national occupational standards
- information on choosing the right assessor qualification
- guidance on who does what in assessment
- help with all the assessment methods
- CPD activities for you and your team
- advice from experienced assessors on what works and what doesn't.

Using the knowledge and experience of a range of contributors and with many real-life examples, this guide is for anyone working towards an assessor qualification.

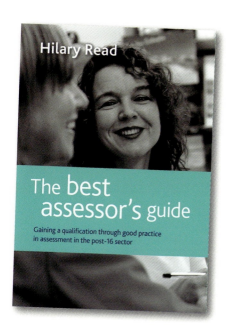

The best quality assurer's guide

A guide to best practice for internal and external quality assurers (IQAs and EQAs).

It contains:

- links to the qualifications for IQAs and EQAs and the national occupational standards
- information on choosing the right IQA and assessor qualification
- guidance on who does what in quality assurance of assessment
- help with sampling and standardisation activities
- CPD activities to use with assessors
- a practical toolkit for IQAs and extra help for Lead IQAs
- advice on how to help centres meet the requirements of the awarding organisation and Ofqual.

Using the knowledge and experience of a range of contributors and with many real-life examples, this guide is for anyone working towards a qualification in quality assurance.

How to order

By phone: Ring the orderline on 0844 888 7138. Lines are open from 9am–9pm Monday to Friday and 9am–5pm Saturday and Sunday.

By post: Fill in the order form below and send your cheque made payable to Read On Publications to: Read On Publications Ltd, PO Box 162, Bideford, Devon, EX39 9DP.

Online: Go to www.readonpublications.co.uk

Downloadable resources

CPD activities for assessors

Twelve practical activities for assessors, linked to the new areas of assessment practice within the QCF.

Activity titles

1 Self-assessment

2 Reflection and CPD

3 The benefits of a holistic approach

4 Keeping it legal

5 Using technology

6 Understanding learning outcomes and assessment criteria

7 Planning for, and minimising, risks

8 Linking assessment to learning

9 Peer and self-assessment

10 Your role in standardisation of assessment

11 Equality, diversity and bilingualism

12 Adapting assessment to meet individual needs

All activities link to the assessment qualifications and the new PTLLS units.

Cost: £15.00 for a single-user licence.

Topics for trainers delivering the assessor qualifications

Nine topics for trainers delivering the assessor qualifications. They comprise slides, session plans and trainer notes, handouts and/or learner activities.

Topic titles

1 CPD and reflective practice for assessors

2 Principles and requirements of assessment

3 Assessment methods

4 Planning assessment

5 Involving the learner

6 Carrying out assessment and reaching decisions

7 Recording and managing information

8 Legal and good practice requirements

9 Quality assurance of assessment

All topics link to the assessment qualifications.

Cost: £250.00 plus VAT for a single-user licence, including photocopying rights.

CPD activities for IQAs

Nine practical activities for IQAs, linked to the new areas of quality assurance of assessment practice within the QCF assessment qualifications.

Activity titles

1 Self-assessment

2 Planning for quality assurance

3 Improving assessment practice

4 Observing assessment practice

5 Evaluating use of technology

6 Running standardisation meetings

7 Continuing professional development (CPD) of assessors

8 Evaluating legal requirements

9 Reflecting on your performance

Cost: £15.00 plus VAT for a single-user licence.

How to order

To purchase a single-user licence, download from www.readonpublications.co.uk. To purchase a multi-user licence for your organisation, email enquiries@readonpublications.co.uk

Order form

To order by post

The best initial assessment guide	£30.00	Quantity	Subtotal £
The best quality assurer's guide	£30.00	Quantity	Subtotal £
The best assessor's guide	£25.00	Quantity	Subtotal £
Excellence in planning and delivering learning	£25.00	Quantity	Subtotal £
All four guides package	£85.00	Quantity	Subtotal £
Three assorted guides package	£75.00	Quantity	Subtotal £
Postage & packing 1–2 guides	£4.90*		Subtotal £
Postage & packing 3–4 guides	£8.00*		Subtotal £

SPECIAL OFFERS

* Postage and packing prices correct at time of going to press but may be subject to change.

Total £

Your details

Title	Name
Job title	
Company	
Address	
	Postcode
Telephone	
Email	

Send your order form and cheque made payable to Read On Publications Ltd to:
Read On Publications Ltd, PO Box 162, BIDEFORD, EX39 9DP

To order online, go to www.readonpublications.co.uk
To order by phone, ring the orderline on 0844 888 7138

Lines are open from 9am–9pm Monday to Friday and 9am–5pm, Saturday and Sunday.